CRASH COURSE
FOR THE GRE

THE PRINCETON REVIEW

Crash Course for the GRE

The Last-Minute Guide to Scoring High

by Karen Lurie

Random House, Inc.
New York

Princeton Review Publishing, L.L.C.
2315 Broadway
New York, NY 10024

E-mail: comments@review.com

Published in the United States by Random House, Inc., New York, and
simultaneously in Canada by Random House of Canada Limited, Toronto.

ISBN 0-375-75325-7

Editor: Lesly Atlas
Designer: Stephanie Martin
Production Editor: Julieanna Lambert
Production Coordinator: Stephanie Martin

Manufactured in the United States of America.

9   8   7   6   5   4   3

ACKNOWLEDGMENTS

The author would like to thank the following people for their help:
Lesly Atlas, Laurie Barnett, John Bergdahl, Jackie Jendras,
Julieanna Lambert, Stephanie Martin, Neil McMahon, and
Jeff Rubenstein.

CONTENTS

INTRODUCTION

ORIENTATION

WHAT IS CRASH COURSE FOR THE GRE?

Crash Course for the GRE is just what it sounds like—a quick but thorough guide to the basic material on the GRE computer-adaptive test (also called the GRE CAT, or GRE computer-based test). It includes helpful techniques for nailing as many questions as possible, even if you don't have a lot of time to prepare. *Crash Course for the GRE* is *not* a comprehensive study guide for the GRE. If you're looking for that, you should try The Princeton Review's *Cracking the GRE CAT*.

WHAT IS THE GRE?

The Graduate Record Examination (GRE) is a multiple-choice aptitude test intended for applicants to graduate schools. It definitely does *not* measure your intelligence, nor does it measure how well you will do in graduate school. The GRE is a test of how well you handle standardized tests.

The three sections of the GRE that count toward your score are (not necessarily in this order):

- one 30-minute, 30-question verbal section

- one 45-minute, 28-question math section

- one 60-minute, 35-question analytic section

The verbal section of the GRE CAT contains four types of questions (in no particular order):

- 8 to 10 antonyms

- 5 to 7 sentence completions

- 6 to 8 analogies

- 2 to 4 reading comprehension passages with a total of 6 to 10 questions

The math section contains two types of questions (in no particular order):

- 13 to 15 quantitative comparisons (with four answer choices)

- 12 to 16 problem-solving questions, including 4 to 6 chart questions from 2 to 3 charts (with five answer choices)

The analytical section contains two types of questions (in no particular order):

- 21 to 25 analytical reasoning (games) questions from 5 to 7 games (each game has 3 or 4 questions)
- 10 to 14 logical reasoning (arguments) questions

Starting in October 1999, there will also be a separate and completely *optional* writing assessment available, which may or may not be recommended by your graduate program as an aid to your application. Check your GRE Registration Booklet or www.gre.org for more information.

Sections That Don't Count

You'll probably have a fourth, unidentified experimental section: another verbal, math, or analytic section. It can be anywhere on the test. This section will not count toward your score. You can't avoid it, and you won't even recognize it. If you get two verbal sections, then one of them is experimental, but you won't know which one. So, don't worry about it. Just do your best on all questions, and plan to be at the test center no longer than four-and-a-half hours.

Occasionally you'll also be required to complete an identified, unscored research section (sometimes called a "pretest"), consisting of additional experimental questions. It will probably be a writing measure or some different math questions. If your test includes this section, it will be last. Fortunately, since you will have completed all scored sections of the test at this point, ETS' use of you as a guinea pig can have no adverse effect on your GRE score. Data obtained from this research section will be used to revise the test over the next few years.

What Does a GRE Score Look Like?

You will receive separate verbal, quantitative, and analytical scores, each on a scale that runs from 200 to 800. GRE scores can rise or fall only by multiples of ten, so the third digit is always zero.

Where Does the GRE Come From?

Like most standardized tests in this country, the GRE is published by the Educational Testing Service (ETS), a big, tax-exempt private company in New Jersey. ETS publishes the GRE under the sponsorship of the Graduate Record Examinations Board, an organization affiliated with the Association of Graduate Schools and the Council of Graduate Schools in the United States.

The GRE isn't written by distinguished professors, renowned scholars, or graduate-school admissions officers. For the most part, it's written by ordinary ETS employees, sometimes with freelance help from local graduate students. There's no reason to be intimidated by these people.

WHY SHOULD I LISTEN TO THE PRINCETON REVIEW?

We monitor the GRE. Our teaching methods for cracking it were developed through exhaustive analysis of all available GREs and careful research into the methods by which standardized tests are constructed. Our focus is on the basic concepts that will enable you to attack any problem, strip it down to its essential components, and solve it in as little time as possible.

GRE CAT FACTS

You can take the GRE CAT on almost any day from October to January, and almost any day during the first three weeks of the months of February through June. You may take the test only once per calendar month. Appointments are scheduled on a first-come, first-served basis. There's no real deadline for registering for the test (technically, you can register the day before), but there's a limited number of seats available on any given day, and centers do fill up, sometimes weeks in advance. It's good to give yourself at least a couple of weeks of lead time to register.

You can schedule a test session for the GRE CAT (which, by the way, will cost you $96) by calling The Sylvan Technologies National Registration Center at (800) GRE-CALL. Or, you can register online at www.gre.org. General inquiries about the GRE can be made by calling Educational Testing Services at (609) 771-7670. You may also call your local test center to set up an appointment (a list of centers is available from ETS; most are Sylvan Learning Centers). In order to schedule your test by phone, you must pay by VISA or Mastercard. Check your GRE Registration Booklet or www.gre.org for more information.

You will receive your scores right after you finish the exam. Scores also go out to schools more quickly than they did for the pencil-and-paper test.

You will never know which questions you missed and how the computer arrived at your final score; you can't verify your final score, learn from your mistakes, or ever see the questions on your test again.

The lack of a physical test booklet makes it impossible to write directly on the problems themselves (to cross out incorrect answers, etc.), but you'll get scratch paper, so your work space is limitless. Your use of scratch paper is one of the keys to scoring well on the GRE CAT.

WHAT THE GRE CAT LOOKS LIKE

When there's a question on the screen, it will look like this:

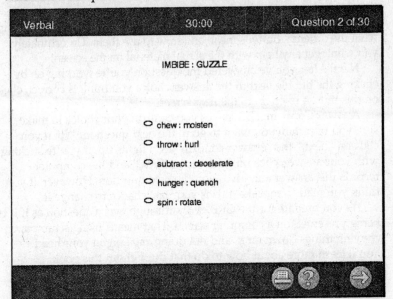

IMBIBE : GUZZLE

○ chew : moisten

○ throw : hurl

○ subtract : decelerate

○ hunger : quench

○ spin : rotate

The problem you're working on will be in the middle of the screen. The answer choices will have little bubbles next to them. To choose an answer, you click on the bubble that corresponds with the choice you are picking.

A readout of the time remaining in the section may be displayed if you choose to do so; the number of questions you've done and the total number of questions in the section will be displayed in the upper right corner. The bottom of the screen will contain the following buttons, from left to right:

Test Exit: You can end the test at any moment by clicking on this button. However, unless you become violently ill, we do not recommend that you ever do this. Even if you decide not to have this test scored (an option you get when you're done with the exam), you should finish the test. After all, it's great practice for when you finally want the test to count. Besides, you can't get a refund from ETS.

Section Exit: You'll be taken out of the section you're working on by clicking on this button, and *you won't get a score*. If you happen to finish a section before the time is up, just sit and rest till the next section begins.

Time: You may opt to display or hide the digital countdown by clicking on this button. Some people like to have it on the screen; others like to look at their watches instead. Whatever you decide, when time is almost up, the display will appear on the screen.

Help: If you click on this button, you'll get a little tutorial explaining what the different buttons mean and how to use them. Unfortunately, you won't get any help with the actual material on the screen!

Next: After you've answered the question you're working on by clicking the bubble next to the answer choice you think is correct, click on this button to go on to the next screen.

Answer Confirm: ETS makes you confirm your choice to make sure you're certain you want to go to the next question. When you click on "next," the "answer confirm" icon lights up. If you're sticking with your answer, click on "answer confirm," and the computer records this answer and gives you the next question. However, if you think you made a mistake, this is your last chance to change it.

As you prepare for the GRE, work through every question as if it is being presented on a computer screen. That means using scrap paper, copying things down on it, and not doing *anything* in your head. You'll learn more about how to do that throughout this book.

Real Tests

You bought *Crash Course for the GRE* because you don't have a lot of time to prepare, and you want the basics. But you still need real GRE questions on which to practice. The only source of real GREs is the publisher of the test, ETS. Therefore, if you have the time, we recommend that you purchase GRE POWERPREP® Software—Test Preparation for the General Test, which includes GRE questions presented in the CAT mode. To order, call the GRE publications office at (800) 537-3160, or order from the web site at www.gre.org.

Stay Current

The information in this book is accurate right now, and will be updated yearly. However, the publishing business is such that if the test changed tomorrow (though it won't), the book might be a little behind. For the most current information possible, obtain ETS' Registration Booklet (you should definitely have one of these). Or, since web sites can be updated daily, visit ETS' web site at www.gre.org, or our web site at www.review.com.

GENERAL STRATEGY

How a Computer-Adaptive Test Works

Computer-adaptive tests use your performance on one question to determine which question you will be asked next. ETS assumes that you have the average score in a particular category—for example, a 480 in verbal. You'll be asked a question of difficulty appropriate to this score level. If you answer correctly, the computer adjusts your score to a new level, say 550, and your next question is more difficult. If you answer incorrectly, your score will drop and your next question will be less difficult. The amount your score will change with each new correct or incorrect answer is reduced as you move further into the test, so by the end of the exam, the computer will have effectively zeroed in on your GRE score. That's the theory, anyway.

So, when you get an answer right, your next question is harder; when you get an answer wrong, your next question is easier. You won't know how you did on the prior question, so just focus on doing your best on each question. *Never, ever try to figure out how difficult a question is supposed to be.*

What Does All This Mean?

It means that how much credit you get for a question depends on how you've done on the previous questions. If you've correctly answered all the questions before it, you're going to get more credit for answering a question correctly than you would if you had missed a bunch of questions before you worked your way to that question. In a nutshell: Your responses to the first questions in a section will have a greater impact on your final score than your responses to those later in the section, after the computer has already determined your score range. Your score moves up and down in larger increments at the beginning of the test than it does toward the end. *The first third to half of each section determines the bulk of your score. So be extra careful on the first third to half of each section.*

Answer Every Question

You will be penalized for not giving an answer to every question in a section. Basically, your raw score will be reduced by the percentage of unanswered questions in a section (e.g., a thirty-question section with six questions left blank will mean a 20 percent reduction of your raw score). *So, do not leave any question unanswered.*

Let the Computer Help You

During the last five minutes of a section, the time display on the computer screen will start flashing, showing you the remaining time in both minutes and seconds. Let this be your signal to start wrapping things up by guessing your favorite letter for whatever questions you have left in the section, since you don't want to leave any questions unanswered in any section.

How to Guess

Because the computer "decides" what to do next based on how you answer the question on the screen, you *must* answer that question. There is no skipping a question and coming back to it later.

Once you've worked carefully through the first third to half of the section, you don't want to get bogged down in time-consuming questions. If you encounter a question that seems extremely difficult or time-consuming, eliminate answers that you know are wrong, and make an educated guess (you're about to learn how). This will allow you to get to subsequent questions, which may be more easily worked, with enough time to work them.

You're probably going to see questions on which you'll have to guess. But we're not talking about random guessing. After all, the right answer is on the screen. ETS doesn't care how you got your answer; it only cares about whether you clicked on the credited response with your mouse. You might as well benefit from this by getting questions right even when you really don't know the answer. And you do that with the Process of Elimination, or POE. POE is your new religion. Learn it. Live it. Love it.

The Amazing Power of POE

There are roughly four times as many wrong answers as there are right answers; it's often easier to identify the wrong answers than to identify the best one. By using POE, you'll be able to improve your score on the GRE by looking for wrong answers instead of right ones on questions you're having trouble with.

Why? Because every time you're able to eliminate an incorrect choice on a GRE question, you improve your odds of finding the best answer. The more incorrect choices you eliminate, the better your odds. Don't be afraid to arrive at ETS' answer *indirectly*. You'll be avoiding the traps laid in your path by the test writers, traps that are designed to catch unwary test-takers who try to approach the problems *directly*.

If you guessed blindly on a five-choice GRE problem, you would have one chance in five of picking ETS' answer. Eliminate one incorrect choice, and your chances improve to one in four. Eliminate three, and you have a fifty-fifty chance of earning points by guessing. Get the picture? You must answer each question to get to the next one, so you'll have to guess sometimes. Why not improve your odds?

Note: Especially on verbal questions, if you're not sure what a word in an answer choice means, don't eliminate that choice. It might be the answer! Only eliminate answers you know are wrong.

The "Best" Answer

The instructions on the GRE tell you to select the "best" answer to each question. ETS calls them "best" answers, or the "credited responses," instead of "correct" answers, to protect itself from the complaints of test-takers who might be tempted to quarrel with ETS' judgment. You have to pick from the choices ETS gives you, and sometimes you might not like any of them. But your job is to find the one answer for which ETS gives credit.

Use That Paper!

For POE to work, it's crucial that you keep track of what choices you're eliminating. By crossing out a clearly incorrect choice, you permanently eliminate it from consideration. If you don't cross it out, you'll keep considering it. Crossing out incorrect choices can make it much easier to find the credited response, because there will be fewer places where it can hide. But how can you cross anything out on a computer screen?

By using your scratch paper! Even though on the GRE, the answer choices have empty bubbles next to them, you're going to pretend that they are labeled A, B, C, D, and E (and so are we, throughout this book). Every time you do a question, you will write down A, B, C, D, E on your scratch paper.

A B C D E	A B C D E	A B C D E	A B C D E
A B C D E	A B C D E	A B C D E	A B C D E

Carve up at least a couple of pages (front and back) like this. This will give you a bunch of distinct work areas per page, which will be especially helpful for the math section; you don't want to get confused when your work from one question runs into your work from a previous question.

Do this and you can physically cross off choices that you're eliminating. Do it every time you do a GRE question, in this book or anywhere else. Get used to writing on scratch paper instead of near the question, since you won't be able to write near the question on test day.

Don't Do Anything in Your Head

Besides eliminating incorrect answers, there are many other ways to use scratch paper to solve questions; you're going to learn them all. Just remember: Even if you're tempted to try to solve questions in your head, even if you think that writing things down on your scratch paper is a waste of time, you're wrong. Trust us. *Always write everything down.*

Read and Copy Carefully

You can do all the calculations right and still get a question wrong. How? What if you solve for x but the question was "What is the value of $x + 3$?" Ugh. Always *reread* the question. Take your time and don't be careless. The question will stay on the screen; it's not going anywhere.

Or, how about this? The radius of the circle is 6, but when you copied the picture onto your scratch paper, you accidentally made it 5. Ugh! Many of the mistakes you will make at first probably stem from copying information down incorrectly. Learn from your mistakes! You have to be extra careful when copying down information.

ACCURACY VS. SPEED

You don't get points for speed; the only thing that matters is accuracy. Take as much time as is necessary to work through each problem carefully (as long as you leave some time at the end of the section to fill out the rest of it). If you miss a question, you'll need to get *at least* the next two right just to get your score back up to where it was before (roughly). But if you're making careless errors, you won't even realize you're missing questions. Get in the habit of double-checking all of your answers before you choose them.

AT THE TESTING CENTER

You'll be asked for two forms of identification; one must be a photo ID. Then an employee will take a digital photograph of you before taking you to the computer station where you will take the test. You get a desk, a computer, a keyboard, a mouse, about six to ten pieces of scratch paper, and a pencil. Before the test begins, make sure your desk is sturdy and you have enough light, and don't be afraid to speak up if you want to move.

If there are other people in the room, they might not be taking the GRE CAT. They could be taking a nursing test, or a licensing exam for architects. And none of the other people will have necessarily started their exams at the same time. The testing center employee will get you set up at your computer, but from then on, the computer itself will act as your proctor. It'll tell you how much time you have left in a section, when time is up, and when to move on to the next section.

The test center employees will be available because they will be monitoring the testing room for security purposes with closed-circuit television. But don't worry, you won't even notice. If you have a question, or need to request more scratch paper during the test, try to do so between the timed sections.

The Tutorial

Before the actual test begins, you'll get an interactive tutorial on how to take the test. Even a computer novice should have no problem with this extremely simple interface. You'll learn how to use the mouse, select an answer, move on to the next question, see how much time you have left in a section, and even stop the test if you need to (but you won't need to). Take as much time as you need to practice each of these functions and get comfortable with your surroundings, the computer and mouse, and the test directions. There's no time limit on the tutorial.

Use the time you have during the tutorial to set up your scratch paper, jot down the step-by-step strategies for each section of the test, and note any math formulas or vocabulary words you always have trouble remembering. You can do whatever you want with this paper and this time, so use them both wisely.

Let It Go

When you begin a new section, focus on that section and put the last one behind you. Don't think about that pesky antonym from an earlier section while a geometry question is on your screen. You can't go back, and besides, your impression of how you did on a section is probably much worse than reality.

This Is the End

When you're done with the test, the computer will ask you twice if you want this test to count. If you say "no," the computer will not record your score, no schools will ever see it, and neither will you. You can't look at your score and then decide whether you want to keep it or not. And you can't change your mind later. If you say you want the test to count, the computer will give you your score right there on the screen. A few weeks later, you'll receive your verified score in the mail (but no copy of the test you took!). You can't change your mind and cancel it.

TEST DAY CHECKLIST

Dress in layers so that you'll be comfortable regardless of whether the room is cool or warm.

Don't bother bringing a calculator; you're not allowed to use one.

Be sure to have breakfast, or lunch, depending on the time for which your test is scheduled (but don't eat anything, you know, "weird"). And go easy on the liquids and caffeine.

Do a few GRE practice problems to warm up your brain. Don't try to tackle difficult new questions, but review a few questions that you've done before to help you review the problem-solving strategies for each section of the GRE CAT. This will also help you put your "game-face" on and get you into test mode.

Make sure to bring two forms of identification (one with a recent photograph) to the test center. Acceptable forms of identification include driver's licenses, photo-bearing employee ID cards, and valid passports.

If you registered by mail, you must also bring the authorization voucher sent to you by ETS.

The Week of the Test

A week before the test is not the time for any major life changes. This is *not* the week to quit smoking, start smoking, quit drinking coffee, start drinking coffee, start a relationship, end a relationship, or quit a job. Business as usual, okay?

PART **II**

TEN STEPS

STEP 1

MAKE A SENTENCE
(ANALOGIES)

What Is an Analogy?

On an analogy, your job is to figure out the relationship between the original pair of words (we'll call them the *stem words*) and find an answer choice in which the words have the same relationship. Let's look at one:

> EVICT : TENANT ::
> ○ patronize : child
> ○ sanction : nation
> ○ enclose : wall
> ○ disbar : lawyer
> ○ ostracize : pariah

The stem words are EVICT and TENANT. What's the relationship?

The Big Technique: Make a Sentence

If you can define both of the stem words, your first step is to make a simple sentence that shows their relationship. Think about defining one in terms of the other, and don't get fancy or tell a story. If you looked up EVICT in the dictionary, and the definition had TENANT in it, what might it say? Something like this: EVICT means to throw out a TENANT. That's your sentence.

The Usual Sentences

A few relationships appear over and over on the GRE. Learn them!

Degree:	ADMIRE : IDOLIZE—IDOLIZE means to ADMIRE a lot.
Type of:	FRUIT : ORANGE—an ORANGE is a type of FRUIT.
Part of:	CHAPTER : BOOK—a CHAPTER is a part of a BOOK.
Function of:	BRAIN : COGNITION—the function of a BRAIN is COGNITION.
Characterized by:	ZEALOT : FERVOR—a ZEALOT is characterized by FERVOR.
With/without:	POOR : MONEY—POOR means without MONEY.

Your Turn

Drill 1

Practice making sentences from the following stem word pairs, defining one word in terms of the other (answers can be found at the end of the chapter):

1. GIGANTIC : LARGE _____
2. FADE : BRILLIANCE _____
3. DICTIONARY : WORDS _____
4. ADHESIVE : BIND _____
5. LETTERS : ALPHABET _____
6. ETERNAL : END _____
7. COTTAGE : HOUSE _____
8. VERSE : POEM _____
9. SYLLABUS : COURSE _____
10. ANTISEPTIC : SANITIZE _____

Write It Down!

If you try to make your sentence in your head, you might forget it after you try a few answer choices or, even worse, change it to agree with one of the answer choices. That defeats the whole purpose!

Always write your sentence on your scratch paper. If you make your sentence from right to left (yes, that's allowed), draw an arrow for that question to remind you to plug in the answer choices from right to left. Then write A, B, C, D, E to represent the five answer choices.

POE

The words in the credited response have to fit exactly in the sentence you made for the original pair of words. If you know the words in the answer choice, and they don't fit into the sentence, eliminate that choice by crossing it off on your scratch paper. If you're not sure you can define the words in an answer choice, don't eliminate that choice. Here's the example again:

EVICT : TENANT ::

- ○ patronize : child
- ○ sanction : nation
- ○ enclose : wall
- ○ disbar : lawyer
- ○ ostracize : pariah

Our sentence was "EVICT means to throw out a TENANT." Let's go to the answer choices:

(A) Is patronize to throw out a child? Nope.

(B) Is sanction to throw out a nation? Nope.

(C) Is enclose to throw out a wall? Nope.

(D) Is disbar to throw out a lawyer? Yes.

(E) Is ostracize to throw out a pariah? Nope, a pariah has already been thrown out.

The best answer is (D).

What If I Don't Know Some of the Words in the Answer Choices?

Let's say you'd never seen the words in answer choice (E) before. How would you know whether they worked in your sentence?

Assuming you knew both stem words, you can still ask yourself whether any word could create a relationship in the choice identical to the relationship in the stem. If not, you can eliminate the choice. Then see what you have left and take an educated guess.

MAKE A SENTENCE, PART 2: WORKING BACKWARD

It's all very nice when you know the stem words. But if you don't know the stem words, you can't make a sentence. So, what should you do?

Since the words in the correct answer choice must have a relationship similar to that of the stem words, they must also have a relationship to each other. So if the words in an answer choice *do not* have a good relationship, that choice cannot be correct.

For example, if you saw "car : seat" in the answer choices, you could get rid of that choice. Why? Because car and seat are not necessarily related. Yes, cars usually have seats, but try making one of those "defining" sentences with car and seat. You can't do it, right? If you looked up "seat" in the dictionary, would "car" be there? Nope. If you looked up "car" in the dictionary, would "seat" be there? Nope.

Your Turn

Drill 2

Decide which of the following pairs have a clear relationship by making sentences with them. If you think a pair of words has no relationship, put an "X" next to that pair. If you don't know the words well enough to tell whether they are related, leave the question blank (answers can be found at the end of the chapter):

1. needle : thread _____
2. vernal : spring _____
3. breach : dam _____
4. dog : cat _____
5. vacillate : steadfast _____
6. scintilla : minuscule _____
7. calumniate : reputation _____
8. sedulous : piquancy _____
9. witty : mordant _____
10. mendacity : truth _____

When You Can't Make a Sentence

So, if you can't make a sentence with the stem words, start by going to the answers and eliminating choices that aren't really related. But what do you do with the answers that are left?

Let's look at an example that's missing a stem word (just pretend it's a word you don't know):

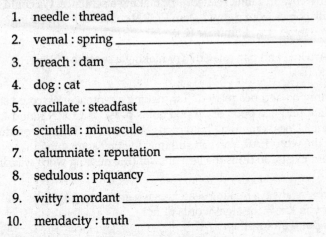

??? : CORN ::
- ◯ flower : stem
- ◯ cube : water
- ◯ cow : milk
- ◯ loaf : pan
- ◯ pod : pea

Since we can't make a sentence with the stem words, we have to go to the answers.

(A) Are flower and stem related? Try making a sentence. We could say "The stem is the base of a flower." Now we take that sentence and work backward with the stem word we know: Can CORN be the base of something? No. That means we can eliminate (A).

(B) Are cube and water related? Try making a sentence. No. Eliminate (B).

(C) Are cow and milk related? Try making a sentence. We could say, "Milk comes from a cow." Does CORN come from something? Not in the same way. Eliminate (C).

(D) Are loaf and pan related? Try making a sentence. Nope. Eliminate (D).

(E) Are pod and pea related? Try making a sentence. We could say, "A pea is found in a pod" or "A pod holds peas." Is CORN found in something? Does something hold corn? Yes, an EAR. Even if you don't think of the word EAR, you can still imagine that something that holds corn exists. So (E) is the best answer (the missing word was, in fact, EAR).

So, you're always making sentences when you do analogies, whether you know the stem words or not.

Let's put it all together.

> INVARIABLE : CHANGE ::
> ○ incurable : disease
> ○ unfathomable : depth
> ○ extraneous : proposition
> ○ ineffable : expression
> ○ variegated : appearance

Your sentence for the relationship between the stem words would be something like "Something INVARIABLE is without CHANGE." Notice that CHANGE is a noun, not a verb. How did we know? We checked the corresponding words in the answer choices. Since disease, depth, proposition, expression, and appearance are nouns, CHANGE must be a noun, too.

(A) Is something incurable without disease? No. Eliminate this choice.

(B) Is something unfathomable without depth? Nope. Eliminate this choice, too.

(C) Is something extraneous without proposition? Do you know the dictionary definition of "extraneous"? Keep this choice and check out the other choices.

(D) Is something ineffable without expression? If you don't know the definition of "ineffable," you'd better keep this choice.

(E) Is something variegated without appearance? Now, we may not know the exact definition of "variegated," but from what we sort of know, it wouldn't fit our sentence. It has something to do with appearance, but it doesn't mean without appearance.

Now we're guessing between choices (C) and (D). Do you think it's more likely that some word means "without proposition" or that some word means "without expression?" (D) is the answer.

Here's another one:

BELIEF : RECANTATION ::
- ○ statement : retraction
- ○ opinion : justification
- ○ doctrine : devotion
- ○ legislation : amendment
- ○ pronouncement : oration

Let's say we're not sure what RECANTATION means. Time to go to the answers.

(A) Are statement and retraction related? Try making a sentence. "Retraction is to take back a statement." Could RECANTATION mean to take back a BELIEF? Maybe, so leave in (A).

(B) Are opinion and justification related? Try making a sentence. Nope. Eliminate (B).

(C) Are doctrine and devotion related? No, but if you weren't sure of the words, you'd have to leave it in.

(D) Are legislation and amendment related? It sounds good, but try making a sentence. Does legislation always have to do with amendments? Nope. Eliminate (D).

(E) Are pronouncement and oration related? No, but if you weren't sure of the words, you'd have to leave it in. The best answer is (A), although some of you might have been guessing (C) or (E), depending on your vocabulary level. It's still better than a blind guess.

The Last Resort

If you've eliminated all the answer choices with words that you know or sort of know, and you're left with a couple of choices containing words that you've never seen before, just guess and move on. Your GRE score is going to be much higher if you are guessing between two choices than it would be if you hadn't eliminated those other three choices by using our techniques.

ANSWERS

Drill 1

1. GIGANTIC means very LARGE.

2. FADE means to lose BRILLIANCE.

3. A DICTIONARY contains WORDS.

4 An ADHESIVE is used to BIND.

5. The ALPHABET is made up of LETTERS.

6. ETERNAL means without END.

7. A COTTAGE is a type of HOUSE.

8. A VERSE is a part of a POEM.

9. A SYLLABUS is a plan for a COURSE.

10. An ANTISEPTIC is used to SANITIZE.

Drill 2

1. A needle pulls thread.

2. Vernal means having to do with spring.

3. A breach is a rift in a dam.

4. Unrelated. Dogs and cats are both pets, but there is no relationship between them.

5. To be steadfast is not to vacillate.

6. A scintilla is a minuscule amount.

7. To calumniate is to ruin the reputation of.

8. Unrelated.

9. To be mordant is to be bitingly witty.

10. Mendacity is not telling the truth.

Step 2

Speak for Yourself
(Sentence Completions)

"I Already Know How to Do These"

Sentence completions—which you've known since kindergarten as fill-in-the-blanks—look very familiar. But beware! The way ETS designs these problems is very different from the way your elementary school teachers did. Here's what a sentence completion looks like:

> Wilson worked _____ on his first
> novel, cloistering himself in his study
> for days on end without food or
> sleep.
>
> ○ carelessly
> ○ creatively
> ○ tirelessly
> ○ intermittently
> ○ voluntarily

Many testers read sentence completions quickly, then go immediately to the choices and begin plugging them into the blanks. This is exactly what ETS wants you to do, so the answer choices will distract you from the meaning of the sentence. This approach may work occasionally on easy problems, but it definitely won't work on more difficult ones. Why take the chance?

The Big Technique: Speak for Yourself

Physically cover the answer choices on the screen, read the sentence, and write down your own words for the blank(s) before you look at the answer choices. This way you won't let the answer choices distract you and thereby play into ETS' hands.

Let's try that sentence completion *without* answer choices:

> Wilson worked _____ on his first
> novel, cloistering himself in his study
> for days on end without food or
> sleep.

Your job is to speak for yourself by filling in the blank with your own word. It doesn't have to be a fancy vocabulary word. It just has to make sense to you in the blank. In this case, the blank is describing the way Wilson worked. Let's use everything we know about the way he worked to help us. We know he's not eating or sleeping, and he's been in his study for days on end (don't worry if you don't know what "cloistering" means). We need a word in the blank that describes working for days on end without food or sleep. How about "hard"? See, it's nothing fancy, but it'll work. So, write down "hard" on your scrap paper (and A, B, C, D, E for eliminating choices, of course).

Now let's bring in the answer choices that went with this question:

○ carelessly
○ creatively
○ tirelessly
○ intermittently
○ voluntarily

All we have to do is go through them, eliminating anything that doesn't mean "hard."

(A) Does "carelessly" mean hard? No. Eliminate.

(B) Does "creatively" mean hard? No. Get rid of this choice.

(C) Does "tirelessly" mean hard? Maybe, since we know that Wilson worked "for days on end without food or sleep." Let's keep this.

(D) Does "intermittently" mean hard? Be careful! Are you sure you know the dictionary definition of the word? If not, keep this choice and continue.

(E) Does "voluntarily" mean hard? Definitely not. Eliminate.

We're down to two possible choices, but we know that "tirelessly" fits, because we know that Wilson worked "for days on end without food or sleep." So the best answer is (C).

Look Before You Leap: The Clue

The clue is the part of the sentence that describes the blank. It's the most descriptive part of the sentence. There was a clue in that sentence that told us how Wilson worked. It was the phrase "days on end." Without it, any number of different words could plausibly fill in the blank. Finding the clue helped us anticipate ETS' answer. Every GRE sentence completion has at least one clue in it. Count on it.

Your Turn

Drill 1

In each of the following sentences, find the clue and underline it. Then write down your own word for the blank. It doesn't matter if your guesses are awkward or wordy. All you need to do is express the right idea.

1. Despite the apparent _____ of the demands, the negotiations dragged on for over a year.

2. Most students found Dr. Schwartz's lecture on art excessively detailed and academic; some thought his display of _____ exasperating.

Drill 2

Now look at the same questions again, this time with the answer choices provided. Use your words above to eliminate answer choices (answers can be found at the end of the chapter):

1. Despite the apparent _____ of the demands, the negotiations dragged on for over a year.
   - (A) hastiness
   - (B) intolerance
   - (C) publicity
   - (D) modesty
   - (E) desirability

2. Most students found Dr. Schwartz's lecture on art excessively detailed and academic; some thought his display of _____ exasperating.
   - (A) pedantry
   - (B) logic
   - (C) aesthetics
   - (D) erudition
   - (E) literalism

Look Before You Leap—Trigger Words and Punctuation

Certain words signal changes in the meaning of a sentence. We call them "trigger words." They provide important structural indicators of the meaning of the sentence, and are often the key to figuring out what words have to mean to fill in the blanks in a sentence completion. Here are some of the most important sentence completion trigger words and punctuation:

but	in contrast
although (though, even though)	unfortunately
unless	heretofore
rather	thus
yet	and
despite	therefore
while	similarly
however	; or :

Paying attention to trigger words is crucial to understanding the meaning of the sentence, thereby helping you to speak for yourself. For example, if your sentence said "Judy was a fair and _____ judge," the placement of the "and" would tell you that the word in the blank would have to be similar to "fair." You could even use the word "fair" as your fill-in-the-blank word.

What if your sentence said, "Judy was a fair but _____ judge"? The placement of the "but" would tell you that the word in the blank would have to be somewhat opposite of "fair," something like "tough."

Let's try this one (we're taking the answer choices away again, for now):

> Although originally created for _____ use, the colorful, stamped tin kitchen boxes of the early twentieth century are now prized primarily for their ornamental qualities.

What's the clue in the sentence that tells us what the boxes were originally created for? Well, we know that they "are now prized primarily for their ornamental qualities." Does this mean that they were originally created for "ornamental" use? No. The trigger word "although" indicates that the word for the blank will mean the opposite of "ornamental." How about "useful"? It may sound strange to say "useful use," but don't worry about how your words sound—it's what they mean that's important.

Now, here are the answer choices:

○ traditional
○ practical
○ occasional
○ annual
○ commercial

(A) Does "traditional" mean useful? No. Eliminate.

(B) Does "practical" mean useful? Yes. But let's just check the remaining choices.

(C) Does "occasional" mean useful? No. Get rid of it.

(D) Does "annual" mean useful? Nope.

(E) Does "commercial" mean useful? No. Eliminate it. The best answer is (B).

Positive/Negative

In some cases, you may think of several words that could go in the blanks. Or, you might not be able to think of any. Rather than spend a lot of time trying to find the "perfect" word, just ask yourself whether the missing word will be a positive word or a negative word. Then write a + or a – symbol on your scratch paper and take it from there. Here's an example (again, without answer choices, for now):

> Trembling with anger, the belligerent colonel ordered his men to _____ the civilians.

Use those clues. We know the colonel is "trembling with anger," and that he's "belligerent" (which means war-like). Is the missing word a "good" word or a "bad" word? It's a "bad" word. The colonel is clearly going to do something nasty to the civilians. Now we can go to the answer choices and eliminate any choices that are positive and therefore couldn't be correct:

- ○ congratulate
- ○ promote
- ○ reward
- ○ attack
- ○ worship

Choices A, B, C, and E are all positive words; therefore, they can all be eliminated. The only negative word among the choices is (D), the best answer.

TWO BLANKS

Many sentence completions will have two blanks rather than just one. The key to getting them right is concentrating on one of the blanks at a time. A two-blank answer choice can be the best answer choice only if it works for both of the blanks. If you can determine that one of the words in the choice doesn't work in its corresponding blank, you can eliminate that choice without checking the other word.

Which blank should you concentrate on? The one which you have a better clue. Once you've decided which blank you have a better clue for, and have written down a word for it, go to the answer choices and look only at the ones provided for that blank. Then eliminate any choice that doesn't work for that blank.

Let's try one:

> A growing number of heretical scientists are claiming the once _____ theory of evolution must be _____, if not actually shelved.

After reading the whole sentence, it seems as if the second blank is easier to start with, because we've got the clue "if not actually shelved" to help us. It tells us that the second blank must mean something like "almost shelved" or "changed in some basically negative way." Now look at the choices, paying attention only to the second word in each (we've deleted the first words to help you ignore them):

○ _____ . . postulated
○ _____ . . popularized
○ _____ . . reexamined
○ _____ . . modified
○ _____ . . promulgated

Eliminate anything that doesn't mean "almost shelved." Choice (B) can definitely go. If you don't know what the words in (A) and (E) mean, you must leave them in. But as far as words we know that would fit with "almost shelved," how about choices (C) and (D)? To "reexamine" or "modify" a theory is to alter it in some way that falls short of actually throwing it out.

Now let's go back to the first blank. If this theory is almost going to be shelved, it's not universally accepted anymore. And, the scientists who want it shelved are heretical, which means they are going against accepted beliefs. The word "once" is in front of the first blank, and we now know that the theory was once universally accepted, because now it isn't. So, let's put "universally accepted" in the first blank. Now look at the first word in the choices we liked, (C) and (D):

○ sacrosanct . . reexamined
○ modern . . modified

There's no reason to believe it's "modern," and "sacrosanct" means "inviolably sacred," or universally accepted. So, the best answer is (C). If we didn't like either of those, we'd check the words that went with (A) and (E), the words we didn't know.

Positive/Negative

Trigger words and punctuation are also especially important on sentence completions with two blanks, which means there will be times you need to use the positive/negative technique to help you speak for yourself.

Trigger words like "although" and "but" show that the relationship between the two blanks involves an opposition (−/+ or +/−). Trigger words like "and" show that the relationship between the two blanks involves a similarity (−/− or +/+). Crossing out choices that don't fit the pattern will help you zero in on the answer.

Although he was usually _____ and
_____ , his illness blunted both his
appetite and his temper.

The trigger word "although" tells us that if his illness blunted both his appetite and his temper now, they both (because of the trigger word "and") must normally be unblunted or extreme. So, both of the words in the blanks will be negative words. Now we can eliminate any choice that has a positive word anywhere in it:

- ◯ gluttonous . . contentious
- ◯ sated . . belligerent
- ◯ avaricious . . responsive
- ◯ eloquent . . reflective
- ◯ ravenous . . reticent

Immediately eliminate choices (C) and (D) because of "responsive" and "eloquent." If you "sort of" know that "sated" is a positive word, eliminate choice (B) also. "Ravenous" would work in the first blank, but "reticent," or quiet, isn't necessarily negative. The best answer is (A). Look up the vocabulary words that you didn't know!

Answers

Drill 2

1. D
2. A

STEP *3*

KNOW THYSELF
(ANTONYMS)

Yes, There Really Are Techniques

You may think that doing well on antonyms, where your sole task is to pick the word opposite in meaning to the stem word, all comes down to vocabulary—that is, if you have a big vocabulary, you'll do well on antonyms, and if you have a tiny vocabulary, you'll have trouble. And yes, the best way to improve your antonym score is to improve your vocabulary, but you don't have much time. Don't worry—we do have techniques that can enable you to squeeze the maximum number of points out of any vocabulary.

The Big Technique: Know Thyself

From now on, think of vocabulary words in terms of these three categories:

Words you know: These are words you can define accurately. If you can't give a definition of a word that's pretty close to what a dictionary would say, then it's not a word you know.

Words you "sort of" know: These are words you've seen or heard before, or maybe even used yourself, but can't define accurately. You may have a sense of how these words are used, but beware! You have to treat these words very differently from the words you can define. After you encounter a word you sort of know in this book, look it up in the dictionary, and make it a word you know from then on.

Words you've never seen before: On every GRE you can expect to see some words you've never seen before. If you've never seen the word in an answer choice, don't eliminate that choice. Focus on the answer choices for which you can define the words.

Your approach to antonyms will vary depending on the type of word that you are dealing with. But you have to be extremely honest with yourself! It's better to be conservative, and to admit that you only "sort of" know a word, than to think you can define a word when you really can't.

Words You Know

When you are absolutely sure that you know what the stem word means, don't just jump at the first choice that looks right. Avoid careless errors by using the following steps:

- As usual, write down A, B, C, D, E on your scratch paper.

- Cover the answer choices on the screen.

- Write down your own simple opposite for the stem word.

- Uncover the answers and use Process of Elimination: Eliminate the answer choices that are nowhere near your own opposite for the stem word. Then, make opposites for the choices that remain and work backwards to the stem word.

Let's try this example:

DISINCLINED·

○ notable
○ gentle
○ willing
○ versatile
○ robust

Let's assume we can define "disinclined." It means something like "not liking." So our own word for the opposite would be something like "liking."

(A) Does "notable" mean liking? Not really; to be sure, what's the opposite of "notable?" Unknown. Does that mean disinclined? Nope.

(B) Does "gentle" mean liking? No. Get rid of it.

(C) Does "willing" mean liking? Maybe. Let's keep it for now

(D) Does "versatile" mean liking? No. Eliminate.

(E) Does "robust" mean liking? No. So the best answer is (C).

Words You "Sort of" Know

First of all, you have to admit it to yourself when you're not sure of the word. If you can't think of a dictionary-like definition, but you've seen it before and could probably use it in a sentence, then you "sort of" know it.

Positive/Negative

Sometimes you can't define a stem word but you do know whether it has a positive or negative connotation. If the stem word has a positive connotation, its antonym has to be negative, so you can eliminate positive answer choices. If the stem word is negative, eliminate negative choices.

Write a + sign down on your scratch paper if the stem word is positive, and a − sign if the stem word is negative. Then write down + or − next to the A, B, C, D, E you've already written down, depending on whether the corresponding word is positive or negative. Don't forget that you're looking for the opposite of the stem.

Let's try using positive/negative on this example:

GARISH:

- ○ adaptable
- ○ understated
- ○ explicable
- ○ generous
- ○ nonchalant

Let's assume you aren't sure what GARISH means, but that you "sort of" know that it's a negative word. That means the antonym must be positive, which, in turn, means that you can eliminate negative answer choices. That eliminates choice (E). Now turn each choice into its opposite and see what you have:

(A) not adaptable

(B) overstated

(C) inexplicable

(D) stingy

As you turn each word into its opposite, compare it to the stem word and determine whether it could mean the same thing.

Could GARISH mean not adaptable? Probably not.

Could GARISH mean overstated? Maybe.

Could GARISH mean inexplicable? Maybe.

Could GARISH mean stingy? Probably not.

If no choice presents itself yet, eliminate the least likely choices, one at a time, and try to zero in on ETS' answer. The best answer is (B).

Let's try another one:

DIGRESS:
- ○ belittle
- ○ confuse
- ○ facilitate
- ○ convince
- ○ focus

Say you're not sure what DIGRESS means, but you know it's negative. That means the antonym must be positive, which, in turn, means that you can eliminate negative answer choices. Choices (A) and (B) are negative, so get rid of them. Next, make opposites for the remaining choices. "Facilitate" means to make easier. Could "digress" mean to "make harder?" Maybe. Could "digress" mean to fail to convince? Maybe. Could "digress" mean to "lose focus"? That's exactly what it means—maybe your memory would be triggered by now. The best answer is (E).

Eliminate Choices That Don't Have Opposites

What's the opposite of chair? What's the opposite of flower? What's the opposite of philosophy?

These words have no clear opposites. If they were choices on an antonym question on the GRE, you could cross them out automatically, even if you didn't know the meaning of the stem word. Why? Because if a choice *has no* opposite, the stem word can't possibly *be* its opposite.

Here's an example:

EXHUME:
- ○ breathe
- ○ inter
- ○ approve
- ○ assess
- ○ facilitate

Let's assume we don't know the meaning of EXHUME. Work through the choices, turning each into its opposite:

(A) Not breathe? Is there really a word for this? There's probably not a direct opposite. Eliminate.

(B) If you don't know this word, don't eliminate it!

(C) Disapprove.

(D) There's no clear opposite. Eliminate.

(E) Make difficult.

You've just improved your guessing odds to one in three. Your chances of finding the best answer now depend on whether narrowing down the choices has made anything click in your minds. The best answer is (B); inter means bury, EXHUME means dig up.

Word Association

Sometimes you're not sure what the stem word means, but you've heard it used with another word or phrase. Use that knowledge to help you eliminate incorrect answer choices. Taking the time to do this may jog your memory of a word's meaning.

DEPLOY:

○ relinquish
○ convert
○ insulate
○ concentrate
○ deceive

You're not exactly sure what DEPLOY means. However, you've probably heard it used in the phrases "deploy missiles" and "deploy troops." Make opposites for the answer choices and plug them into your phrase.

(A) Does "hold onto missiles" make any sense? Maybe.

(B) Does "remain unchanged missiles" make any sense? Nope.

(C) Does "expose missiles" make any sense? Maybe.

(D) Does "spread out missiles" make any sense? Yes.

(E) Does "remain truthful to missiles" make any sense? Nope.

This technique usually won't eliminate all of the incorrect answer choices, but it can help you narrow them down.

Let's try again:

HEDGE:

- ○ attack repeatedly
- ○ risk commitment
- ○ seek advantage
- ○ lose pressure
- ○ become interested

You've probably heard the phrase "to hedge your bets."

(A) There is no direct opposite for "attack repeatedly." Eliminate.

(B) Does "not risk commitment (with) your bets" make sense? Sure. Keep this choice.

(C) Does "not seek advantage (with) your bets" make sense? Maybe.

(D) Does "gain pressure (with) your bets" make sense? Huh? Eliminate.

(E) Does "become uninterested (in) your bets" make sense? Probably not.

Now that we're down to two choices, do you think it's more likely that "to hedge your bets" means to not take risks, or to not seek advantage? The best answer is (B). To hedge a bet is to counterbalance it with other transactions so as to limit risk.

Secondary Meanings

HEDGE is an example of a word that means something different as a noun than it does as a verb. ETS likes to use the secondary meanings of words—in other words, the meaning of the word that doesn't come to your mind right away. Isn't that just like them? How would you have known that they wanted the verb meaning of HEDGE? You'd have checked the answer choices—if they're all verbs, then so is the stem. Besides, what's the opposite of *a hedge*?

Combine Techniques

Don't be afraid to combine all of these techniques. Sometimes you can eliminate a couple of choices by using positive/negative, then use word association on the choices that remain. Don't forget to work backward when you are down to two choices.

Words You've Never Seen Before

Quickly make an opposite for each answer choice. Eliminate any answer choice that doesn't have a clear, direct opposite. Guess the most extreme answer choice you have left. Then move on! Don't spend too much time on words you don't know. Know when to fold 'em.

STEP 4

TREASURE HUNT
(READING COMPREHENSION)

THE COMMON DENOMINATOR

Reading comprehension is the one thing common to almost every standardized test. You've seen it before: a passage about something pretty boring, followed by questions. On the GRE, there are two basic types of passages: science and non-science. The science passages may be either specific or general. Non-science passages will be about either humanities or social studies topics.

Sample Passage

We will refer again and again to the following sample passage:

It is well known that termites are blind, but little has been discovered about the other sense organs of these insects or their reactions to various stimuli. Body odors, as well as odors related to sex and to colony, certainly play a part in the activities of the termite colony. When specimens of eastern subterranean termites are placed in a jar containing a colony of rotten wood termites from the Pacific Coast, the host termites recognize these foreign insects by differences in odor and eventually kill the invaders. The progress of the chase and kill is very slow, and the larger host termites appear awkward in their efforts to bite and kill their smaller but quicker-moving cousins. Finally, more or less by sheer numbers and by accident, they corner and exterminate the enemy.

Eastern dealated (wingless) termites that manage to survive in the rotten wood termite colony for more than a week, however, are no longer molested. This is noteworthy, since eastern termites of this variety had previously been pursued and killed. Fresh eastern wingless specimens placed in the colony alongside the week-old visitors are immediately attacked, thus indicating that the rotten wood termites have in no way lost their capacity for belligerence.

What else besides odor helps termites interpret the world around them? The insects have sense or "chorodontal" organs located on the antennae, on the bristles, on the base of the mandibles, and on the legs. These organs apparently enable termites to receive vibrations sent through the air, or, more precisely, aid in the reception of stimuli sent through the nest material or through air pockets within the nest material. When alarmed, soldier termites exhibit synchronous, convulsive movements that appear to be a method of communication adapted to the chorodontal organ system, although no sound that is audible to man is produced by these movements. Termite soldiers also strike their heads against wood and other nest materials, producing noises that, after passing through the sounding board formed by the nest material, become rustling and crackling sounds plainly audible to man's duller and possibly differently attuned perceptions. In fact, soldiers of one termite species, found in the arid regions of California, strike their heads against the dry, dead flower stalks of Spanish bayonets and agave plants with such force that the sound produced can be heard several feet away. Other types of soldier termites found in the tropics make audible clicking noises with their jaws.

There is a clear correlation between the functioning of the chorodontal system and termite settlement patterns. Seldom are termites found infesting railroad ties over which there is frequent heavy traffic, or on the woodwork of mill or factory buildings where heavy machinery in motion would cause vibrations. Small-scale tests with a radio speaker and vibrator yielded interesting results when termites were placed in the speaker and exposed to various frequency vibrations. When the vibrations ranged from 50–100 per second, the termites were thrown about; at vibrations of 100–500, termites set their feet and mandibles and held on with all their power; at 2,000–5,000 vibrations per second, the termites crawled about undisturbed.

Most testers read much too slowly and carefully on reading comps, trying to memorize all the details crammed into the passage. When they reach the end of the passage, they often gulp and realize they have no idea what they have just read. They've wasted a lot of time and gotten nothing out of it.

THE BIG TECHNIQUE: TREASURE HUNT

On the GRE, you read for one reason only: to earn points. The questions test only a tiny fraction of the boring, hard-to-remember details that are packed into each passage. So don't try to read and remember everything in the passage. Treat it like a treasure hunt and just look for the information that answers the questions.

Do this by *not* reading every word of the passage. Just spend a few minutes skimming it, focusing on the first and last sentence of each paragraph of the passage, and noting on your scratch paper the main idea or theme of the passage as a whole, and anything you think is important about the way the information is presented. In other words, case the joint—get familiar with the passage. Quickly.

Don't try to memorize what you're reading, or to learn any of the supporting details. All you should be doing is looking for a general sense of the overall passage which can be reduced to a few simple words. Remember, the passage isn't going anywhere. It will be on the screen until you answer the question. You don't have to memorize anything.

Finding the Main Idea: A Test Drive

Try this technique on our sample passage. You should come away with the main idea of "all about termite senses." Scrawl a quick note—"termite senses"—on your scratch paper.

Attack the Questions

There are two types of questions: specific and general. Because most of the questions you see will be specific, we're going to discuss specific questions first.

Specific Questions

Specific questions are ones that concern specific details in the passage. You should go back to the passage to find exactly what the passage said for each specific detail question. (See, it's a treasure hunt!) Skim the passage quickly to find where that detail is discussed.

Most specific questions will have what we call a lead word or phrase. These are words or phrases that will be easy to skim for in the passage, such as "The author mentions mayonnaise in order to . . ." (the lead word is "mayonnaise").

Here's What You Do

Identify the lead word or phrase in the question. They will be the most descriptive words in the question.

Quickly skim the passage to find that word or phrase.

Scroll so that the lead words are in the middle of the screen. This should put the part of the passage that must be paraphrased to answer the question right next to the answer choices. If this doesn't do it, look for the next occurrence of the lead words and repeat the process.

Read the question again and answer it in your own words, based on the information you found in the passage.

Then use POE.

Some specific questions have line references in them, such as, "The author uses the term 'indigenous labor' (line 40) to mean . . . " Since ETS isn't likely to send you directly to the answer, you should always:

Scroll so that the line number is in the middle of the screen.

Read at least five lines before and five lines after the line number you're referred to. That's where the answer will be.

Read the question again and answer it in your own words, based on the information you found in the passage.

Then use POE.

POE and the Answer Choices

This is a treasure hunt; in other words: *The answers are in the passage.* Don't pick any extreme answers. Keep everything moderate and stick to the scope of the passage. Don't bring any outside knowledge you might happen to have on the subject. Stay in the world of the passage; that's where you'll find the treasure.

Let's try a question from our sample passage:

> It can be inferred from the passage that dealated eastern termites that have survived a week in a rotten wood termite colony are no longer attacked because they
>
> ○ have come to resemble the rotten wood termites in most ways
>
> ○ no longer have an odor provocative to the rotten wood termites
>
> ○ no longer pose a threat to the host colony
>
> ○ have learned to resonate at the same frequency as the host group
>
> ○ have changed the pattern in which they use their mandibles

"Dealated termites"—those are your lead words. Check the passage—they are first mentioned in the first sentence of the second paragraph. By skimming that paragraph, and a few sentences in the previous one, we see that we're looking for an answer choice that has to do with odor.

(A) This statement is not supported in the passage. While it may be true that the dealated termites have come to resemble the hosts in one way, there is nothing in the passage to suggest that they have come to resemble them in most ways. Eliminate.

(B) This sounds like just what we're looking for. A good possibility.

(C) The foreign termites didn't pose a threat in the first place; all they really did was smell funny. Eliminate.

(D) Making sounds has not yet been mentioned in the passage. Eliminate.

(E) A nutty choice, unsupported by the passage. Eliminate. The best answer is (B).

Let's try another one:

> According to the passage, a termite's jaw can be important in all of the following EXCEPT
>
> ○ aggression against intruders of other termite species
> ○ the reception of vibrations sent by other termites
> ○ stabilization of the insect against physical disturbances
> ○ the production of sound made by striking wood or plants
> ○ sounding an alert to notify other termites of danger

On an EXCEPT question, your job is to pick the answer that is incorrect, which means the other four answers are correct and *can* be found in the passage. Keep that in mind:

(A) The first paragraph says that termites kill intruders by biting them. This statement is correct. Eliminate.

(B) The second sentence in the third paragraph says that some of a termite's chorodontal organs are located on its mandibles, or jaws. This statement is correct. Eliminate.

(C) The final sentence of the passage says that termites "set their . . . mandibles" when subjected to certain physical disturbances. This statement is correct. Eliminate.

(D) Termites strike wood and plants with their heads, not their jaws. This statement appears to be incorrect, and therefore a strong possibility.

(E) The final sentence of the third paragraph describes termites making a sound with their jaws. This sentence is part of a discussion of how termites communicate with other termites "when alarmed." This statement is correct. Eliminate. The best answer is (D).

See how we're using the passage to answer the questions? That's because it's a treasure hunt! Let's try another one:

It can be inferred from the passage that an insecticide designed to confuse soldier termites would be most effective if it deprived the insect of its

○ eyes

○ ears

○ bristles

○ wings

○ odor

Go back and look for the answer. Soldier termites are mentioned in the third paragraph. Then check the choices:

(A) Termites are blind. Eliminate.

(B) There's no mention of ears in the passage. For all we know, termites don't have them. Eliminate.

(C) Bristles are part of a termite's chorodontal system. A possibility.

(D) No mention of wings, which have nothing to do with senses. Eliminate.

(E) We've just been talking about odor. Odorless termites might confuse soldier termites. But why would depriving a soldier termite of its own odor confuse it? (C) seems a better choice.

General Questions

General questions are ones that ask about the main idea, the theme, or the tone of the passage, as a whole. There is no single place in the passage to find the answers to these questions. But the answer is probably on your scratch paper—you've already jotted down your impression of the main idea.

General questions will almost always have general answers. That means that you can eliminate any choice that is too specific (of course you'll write A, B, C, D, E down on your scratch paper for this purpose). Nor will the main idea of a passage ever be something that could not possibly be accomplished in a few short paragraphs. (The author's purpose in writing a 250-word essay could never be "to explain the meaning of life.") The incorrect choices on a question like this will probably be statements that are partly true, or are true of part of the passage but not of the whole thing. Let's try one, using our termite passage:

> The author's primary concern in the passage is to
> - ○ show how little is known of certain organ systems in insects
> - ○ describe the termite's method of overcoming blindness
> - ○ provide an overview of some termite sensory organs
> - ○ relate the termite's sensory perceptions to man's
> - ○ describe the termite's aggressive behavior

A "primary concern" is pretty much the same thing as a "main idea" or "main theme" or "author's purpose." Check out each choice without looking back at the passage. Why? Because the details in the passage may lead you astray. The main idea you wrote on your scratch paper should be enough to lead you to the best answer.

(A) Termites are insects, but the passage is not about insects; it is about termites. This choice can be eliminated for that reason alone. If the main purpose of a passage is to describe a particular person or thing, then that particular person or thing will definitely be mentioned specifically in ETS' answer. If you have a passage about Charles Dickens, its main purpose will not be to "discuss the works of English novelists." Similarly, if the main purpose of a passage is to describe something about termites, then on a main idea question you can eliminate any choice that contains no mention of termites. So eliminate this choice.

(B) Common sense alone tells you that termites have no methods of "overcoming blindness." Eliminate.

(C) This corresponds closely with the main idea we discovered. Hang on to this choice. It's a possibility.

(D) We can tell from our quick search for the main idea that the author's primary concern is not a comparison between termites and humans. Eliminate.

(E) This choice makes no mention of senses. The passage touches on fighting, but not as the main idea. Eliminate. The best answer is (C).

STEP 5

MATH VOCABULARY
(NUMBERS)

It's a Reading Test

ETS says that the math section of the GRE tests the "ability to reason quantitatively and to solve problems in a quantitative setting." Translation: It mostly tests how much you remember from the math courses you took in seventh, eighth, and ninth grades. That means good news for you: GRE math is easier than SAT math. As you might know, many people study little or no math in college. If the GRE tested "college-level" math, everyone but math majors would bomb. So, junior high it is. By brushing up on the modest amount of math you need to know for the test, you can significantly increase your GRE math score.

So, ETS is limited to the math that nearly everyone has studied: arithmetic, basic algebra, basic geometry, and basic statistics. There's no calculus (or even precalculus), no trigonometry, and no major-league algebra or geometry. Because of these limitations, ETS has to resort to tricks and traps in order to create hard problems. Even the most difficult GRE math problems are typically based on pretty simple principles; what makes some difficult is that the simple principles are disguised. In a way, this is more of a reading test than a math test.

The Big Technique: Math Vocabulary

Vocabulary in the math section? Well, if the math section is just a reading test, then in order to understand what you read, you have to know the language, right?

Quick—what's an integer? Is 0 even or odd? How many even prime numbers are there? These terms look familiar, but it's been a while, right? Let's review:

1. **consecutive**—Integers listed in order of increasing value without any integers missing in between. For example: $-3, -2, -1, 0, 1, 2, 3$.

2. **decimals**—When you're adding or subtracting decimals, just pretend you're dealing with money. Simply line up the decimal points and proceed as you would if the decimal points weren't there:

$$34.500$$

$$87.000$$

$$123.456$$

$$+ \ \underline{\ \ 0.980\ }$$

$$245.936$$

Subtraction works the same way:

$$17.66$$

$$- \ \underline{\ \ 3.20\ }$$

$$14.46$$

To multiply, just do it as if the decimal points weren't there, and then put the point in afterwards, counting the total number of digits to the right of the decimal points in the numbers you are multiplying, and then placing the decimal point in your solution so that you have the same number of digits to the right of it:

$$3.451$$

$$\times \ \underline{\ \ 8.9\ }$$

$$30.7139$$

Except for placing the decimal point, we did exactly what we would have done if we had been multiplying 3,451 and 89.

To divide, set up the problem as a fraction, then move the decimal point all the way to the right. You must then move the decimal point in the other number the same number of spaces to the right. For example:

$$\frac{24}{1.25} = \frac{2400}{125} = 19.2$$

3. **denominator**—The bottom number in a fraction.

4. **difference**—The result of subtraction.

5. **digit**—The numbers 0, 1, 2, 3, 4, 5, 6, 7, 8, and 9. Just think of them as the numbers on your phone dial. The number 189.75 has five digits: 1, 8, 9, 7, and 5. Five is

the hundredths digit, 7 is the tenths digit, 9 is the units digit, 8 is the tens digit, and 1 is the hundreds digit.

6. **divisible**—Capable of being divided with no remainder. An integer is divisible by 2 if its units digit is divisible by 2. An integer is divisible by 3 if the sum of its digits is divisible by 3. An integer is divisible by 5 if its units digit is either 0 or 5. An integer is divisible by 10 if its units digit is 0.

7. **even/odd**—An even number is any integer that can be divided evenly by 2 (like 4, 8, and 22); any integer is even if its units digit is even. An odd number is any integer that can't be divided evenly by 2 (like 3, 7, and 31); any integer is odd if its units digit is odd. Even + even = even; odd + odd = even; even + odd = odd; even × even = even; odd × odd = odd; even × odd = even. Don't confuse odd and even with positive and negative. Fractions are neither even nor odd.

8. **exponent**—Exponents are a sort of mathematical shorthand. Instead of writing (2)(2)(2)(2) we can write 2^4. The little 4 is called an "exponent" and the big 2 is called a "base."

HERE ARE SOME RULES ABOUT EXPONENTS

Raising a number greater than 1 to a power greater than 1 results in a bigger number. For example, $2^2 = 4$.

Raising a fraction between 0 and 1 to a power greater than 1 results in a smaller number. For example, $\left(\frac{1}{2}\right)^2 = \frac{1}{4}$.

A negative number raised to an even power becomes positive. For example, $(-2)^2 = 4$.

A negative number raised to an odd power remains negative. For example, $(-2)^3 = -8$.

When you see a number raised to an negative exponent, just put a 1 over it and get rid of the negative sign. For example, $(2)^{-2} = \left(\frac{1}{2}\right)^2$, which $= \frac{1}{4}$.

You probably won't have to worry about adding or subtracting exponents, but you might be asked to multiply or divide. Just remember this phrase: *When in doubt, expand it out*. In other words:

$$2^2 \times 2^4 = (2 \times 2)(2 \times 2 \times 2 \times 2) = 2 \times 2 \times 2 \times 2 \times 2 \times 2 = 2^6$$

Same thing with division:

$$2^6 \div 2^2 = (2 \times 2 \times 2 \times 2 \times 2 \times 2) \div (2 \times 2) = 2 \times 2 \times 2 \times 2 = 2^4$$

And don't forget PEMDAS (if you don't remember what PEMDAS is, see number 16):

$$(4^5)^2 = (4 \times 4 \times 4 \times 4 \times 4)(4 \times 4 \times 4 \times 4 \times 4) = 4 \times 4 \times 4 \times 4 \times 4 \times 4 \times 4 \times 4 \times 4 \times 4 = 4^{10}$$

9. **factor**—a is a factor of b if b can be divided by a without leaving a remainder. For example, 1, 2, 3, 4, 6, and 12 are all factors of 12.

10. **fractions**—A fraction is just a shorthand for division. On the GRE you'll probably be asked to compare, add, subtract, multiply, and divide them. In multiplication, you just go straight across:

$$\frac{4}{5} \times \frac{2}{3} = \frac{8}{15}$$

In division, you multiply by the second fraction's reciprocal; in other words, turn the second fraction upside down (that is, put its denominator over its numerator), then multiply:

$$\frac{4}{5} \div \frac{2}{3} = \frac{4}{5} \times \frac{3}{2} = \frac{12}{10} = \frac{6}{5}$$

If you were asked to compare $\frac{3}{7}$ and $\frac{7}{14}$, all you have to do is multiply diagonally up from each denominator, as shown:

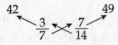

Now, just compare 42 to 49. Since 49 is bigger, that means $\frac{7}{14}$ is the bigger fraction. This technique is called the *Bowtie*. You can also use the Bowtie to add or subtract fractions with different denominators (because to add or subtract, the fractions need the same denominator). Just multiply the denominators of the two fractions, and then multiply diagonally up from each denominator, as shown:

$$\frac{3}{4} + \frac{2}{7} = \overset{21}{\frac{3}{4}} \times \overset{8}{\frac{2}{7}} = \frac{21}{28} + \frac{8}{28} = \frac{29}{28}$$

$$\frac{3}{4} - \frac{2}{7} = \overset{21}{\frac{3}{4}} \times \overset{8}{\frac{2}{7}} = \frac{21}{28} - \frac{8}{28} = \frac{13}{28}$$

If the denominators are the same, you don't need the Bowtie. You just keep the same denominator and add or subtract the numerators:

$$\frac{1}{9} + \frac{2}{9} + \frac{4}{9} = \frac{1+2+4}{9} = \frac{7}{9}$$

$$\frac{7}{9} - \frac{4}{9} - \frac{2}{9} = \frac{7-4-2}{9} = \frac{1}{9}$$

11. **integer**—The integers are the "big places" on the number line: –5, –4, –3, –2, –1, 0, 1, 2, 3, 4, 5, 6. Note that fractions, such as $\frac{1}{2}$, are not integers.

12. **median**—The middle value in a set of numbers, above and below which lie an equal number of values. Just think "median = middle." For example, the median in the set {1, 2, 4, 5, 0, 3, 7} is 5.

13. **mode**—The mode is the number or range of numbers in a set that occurs the most frequently. Just think "mode = most." For example, the mode in the set {1, 3, 6, 4, 7, 5, 3, 2, 4, 3} is 3.

14. **multiple**—A multiple of a number is that number multiplied by an integer other than 0. –20, –10, 10, 20, 30, 40, 50, and 60 are all multiples of 10.

15. **numerator**—The top number in a fraction.

16. **order of operations**—Also known as PEMDAS, or Please Excuse My Dear Aunt Sally. Parentheses > Exponents > Multiplication = Division > Addition = Subtraction. This is the order in which the operations are to be performed. For example:

$$10 - (6 - 5) - (3 + 3) - 3 =$$

Start with the parentheses. The expression inside the first pair of parentheses, $6 - 5$, equals 1. The expression inside the second pair equals 6. Now rewrite the problem as follows:

$$10 - 1 - 6 - 3 =$$
$$9 - 6 - 3 =$$
$$3 - 3 =$$
$$= 0$$

Here's another example:

Say you were asked to compare $(3 \times 2)^2$ and $(3) (2^2)$. $(3 \times 2)^2 = 6^2$, or 36, and $(3) (2^2) = 3 \times 4$, or 12.

Note that with multiplication and division, you just go left to right (hence the "=" sign in the description of PEMDAS above). Same with addition and subtraction. In other words, if the only operations you have to perform are multiplication and division, you don't have to do all multiplication first, because they are equivalent operations. Just go left to right.

17. **permutation**—A permutation is an arrangement of things in a definite order. You may remember the word "factorial." Four factorial, or $4! = 4 \times 3 \times 2 \times 1$, which is 24. For example, to figure out how many different ways you could arrange five books on a shelf, you multiply $5 \times 4 \times 3 \times 2 \times 1$, or 120. A *combination* is a permutation in which order doesn't matter.

18. **positive/negative**—Positive integers get bigger as they move away from 0 (6 is bigger than 5); negative inte-

gers get smaller as they move away from zero (–6 is smaller than –5). Positive × positive = positive; negative × negative = positive; positive × negative = negative. Be careful not to confuse positive and negative with odd and even.

19. **prime**—A prime number is a number that is evenly divisible only by itself and by 1. Zero and 1 are not prime numbers, and 2 is the only even prime number. Other prime numbers include 3, 5, 7, 11, and 13 (but there are many more).

20. **probability**—Probability is equal to the outcome you're looking for divided by the total outcomes. If it is impossible for something to happen, the probability of it happening is equal to 0. If something is certain to happen, the probability is equal to 1. If it is possible for something to happen, but not necessary, the probability is between 0 and 1, otherwise known as a fraction. For example, if you flip a coin, what's the probability that it will land on "heads"? One out of two, or $\frac{1}{2}$. What is the probability that it won't land on "heads"? One out of two, or $\frac{1}{2}$. If you flip a coin nine times, what's the probability that the coin will land on "heads" on the tenth flip? One out of two, or $\frac{1}{2}$. Previous flips do not affect anything.

21. **product**—The result of multiplication.

22. **quotient**—The result of division.

23. **reciprocal**—The inverse of something; the reciprocal of $\frac{1}{2}$ is $\frac{2}{1}$.

24. **reducing fractions**—To reduce a fraction, "cancel" or cross out factors that are common to both the numerator and the denominator. For example, to reduce $\frac{18}{24}$ just divide both 18 and 24 by the biggest common factor, 6. That leaves you with $\frac{3}{4}$. If you couldn't think of

6, both 18 and 24 are even, so just start cutting them in half (or by thirds) till you can't go any further. And remember—you cannot reduce across an equal sign (=), a plus sign (+), or a minus sign (−).

25. **remainder**—The remainder is the number left over when one integer cannot be divided evenly by another. The remainder is always an integer. Remember grade school math class? It's the number that came after the big "R."

26. **square root**—The sign $\sqrt{}$ indicates the square root of a number. For example, $\sqrt{2}$ means that something squared equals 2. You can't add or subtract square roots unless they have the same number under the root sign ($\sqrt{2} + \sqrt{3}$ does *not* equal $\sqrt{5}$, but $\sqrt{2} + \sqrt{2} = 2\sqrt{2}$). You can multiply and divide them just like regular integers:

$$\sqrt{2} \times \sqrt{3} = \sqrt{6}$$
$$\sqrt{6} \div \sqrt{3} = \sqrt{2}$$

By the way, here are a few square roots to remember that might come in handy:

$$\sqrt{1} = 1$$
$$\sqrt{2} = 1.4$$
$$\sqrt{3} = 1.7$$
$$\sqrt{4} = 2$$

Note: if you're told that $x^2 = 16$, then $x = \pm 4$. You must be especially careful to remember this on quantitative comparison questions. But if you're asked for the value $\sqrt{16}$ you are being asked for the positive root only, so the answer is 4. A square root is always positive.

27. **standard deviation**—The standard deviation of a set is a measure of the set's variation from its mean. You'll rarely, if ever, have to actually calculate it, so just remember this: The bigger the standard deviation, the more widely dispersed the values are. The smaller the standard deviation, the more closely grouped the values in a set are around the mean. For example, the

standard deviation of the numbers 6, 0, and 6 is bigger than the standard deviation of the numbers 4, 4, and 4, because 6, 0, and 6 are more widely dispersed than 4, 4, and 4.

28. **sum**—The result of addition.

29. **zero**—An integer that's neither positive nor negative, but is even. The sum of 0 and any other number is that other number; the product of 0 and any other number is 0.

QUANTITATIVE COMPARISON

There are two question formats on the math section: five-choice problem-solving questions, and four-choice quantitative comparisons (or quant comps). A quant comp is a math question that consists of two quantities, one in Column A and one in Column B. You are to compare the two quantities and choose:

(A) if the quantity in Column A is *always* greater

(B) if the quantity in Column B is *always* greater

(C) if the quantities are *always* equal

(D) if *different* numbers would result in *different* answers.

In this book, we're going to phrase the answer choices exactly that way, though on your test it will be slightly different (but it will mean the same thing).

Quant comps have only four answer choices. That's great: A blind guess has one chance in four of being correct. Always write A, B, C, D (but no E) on your scratch paper so you can cross off wrong answer choices as you go. The content of quant comp problems is drawn from the same basic arithmetic, algebra, and geometry concepts that are used on GRE math problems in other formats. In general, then, you'll apply the same techniques that you use on other types of math questions. Still, quant comps do require a few special techniques of their own.

The Peculiar Behavior of Choice (D)

Any problem containing only numbers must have a single solution. Therefore, the fourth bubble, or choice (D), can be eliminated immediately on all such problems. For example:

Column A	Column B
$\frac{2}{3}$	$\frac{3}{4}$

○ the quantity in Column A is always greater
○ the quantity in Column B is always greater
○ the quantities are always equal
○ different numbers would result in different answers

You know the answer can be determined, so the answer could never be choice (D). So right off the bat, as soon as you see a quant comp that involves only numbers, you can eliminate (D) on your scratch paper. The answer to this one is (B), by the way. Use the Bowtie, so you end up with 8 versus 9.

It's Not What It *Is*, But Which Is *Bigger*

You don't always have to figure out what the exact values would be in both columns before you compare them. The prime directive is to compare the two columns. Finding ETS' answer is frequently merely a matter of simplifying, reducing, factoring, or unfactoring. For example:

Column A	Column B
$\frac{1}{17} + \frac{1}{8} + \frac{1}{5}$	$\frac{1}{5} + \frac{1}{17} + \frac{1}{7}$

○ the quantity in Column A is always greater
○ the quantity in Column B is always greater
○ the quantities are always equal
○ different numbers would result in different answers

The first thing to do is eliminate choice (D), because there are only numbers here. Then, notice that there are fractions in common to both columns; both contain $\frac{1}{17}$ and $\frac{1}{5}$. If the same numbers are in both columns, they can't make a difference to the total quantity. So just cross them off (after copying down the problem on your scratch paper, of course). Now, what's left? In Column A we have $\frac{1}{8}$, and in Column B we have $\frac{1}{7}$. All we have to do now is compare $\frac{1}{8}$ to $\frac{1}{7}$. Use the Bowtie and we get choice (B).

STEP 6

DRAW IT YOURSELF
(FIGURES)

FIRST, LET'S WARM UP

If there's one type of math that most people don't tend to use in real life, it's geometry. So, first, here's some more math vocabulary for you to bone up on:

1. **arc**—An arc is a section of the outside, or circumference, of a circle. An angle formed by two radii is called a central angle (it comes out to the edge from the center of the circle). There are 360 degrees in a circle, so if there is an arc formed by, say, a 60-degree central angle, and 60 is one-sixth of 360, then the arc formed by this 60-degree central angle will be one-sixth of the circumference of the circle:

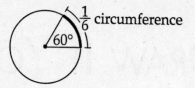

2. **circle**—A circle contains 360 degrees. The area of a circle is π times the square of the radius ($A = \pi r^2$).

3. **circumference**—The circumference of a circle is the distance around the outside. Circumference is 2 times π times the radius ($2\pi r$), or π times the diameter (πd). For example, if a circle has a radius of 4, and $C = (2\pi r)$, that circle has a circumference of 8π.

4. **coordinate geometry**—This involves a grid, like the one on the next page, where the horizontal line is the x-axis and the vertical line is the y-axis.

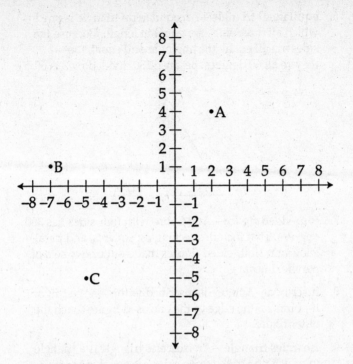

Point *A* on the diagram above is (2,4) because the x-coordinate is 2 over from the origin (0,0) and the y-coordinate is 4 above the origin. Point *B* is (–7,1). Point *C* is (–5,–5).

5. **diameter**—A straight line segment passing through the center of a circle; also, twice the length of the radius. In this circle, the diameter is 6:

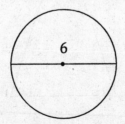

6. **equilateral triangle**—An equilateral triangle is one in which all three sides are equal in length. Because the sides are all equal, the angles are all equal, too— they're all 60 degrees, because 180 divided by 3 is 60:

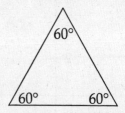

7. **four-sided figure**—Any figure with four sides has 360 degrees. That includes rectangles, squares, and parallelograms (four-sided figures made out of two sets of parallel lines).

8. **inscribed**—A figure is inscribed within another figure if points on the edge of the enclosed figure touch the outer figure.

9. **isosceles triangle**—An isosceles triangle is a triangle in which two of the three sides are equal in length. This means that two of the angles are also equal, and that the third angle is not:

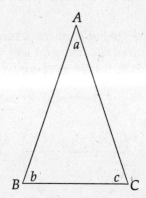

$AB = AC$ and angle b = angle c

10. **line**—A line (which can be thought of as a perfectly flat angle) is a 180-degree angle.

11. **parallel lines**—Lines which never meet. When two parallel lines are cut by a third line, only two different angles are formed: big angles and small angles. All the big angles are equal. All the small angles are equal. The sum of *any* big and *any* small angle is always 180 degrees (the sum of the degrees of a line):

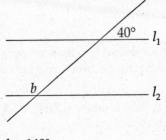

$b = 140°$

12. **parallelogram**—A four-sided figure made from two sets of parallel lines. The opposite angles are equal, and the big angle plus the small angle add up to 180 degrees:

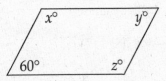

$x = 120°, y = 60°, z = 120°$

13. **perimeter**—The perimeter of a rectangle, square, parallelogram, triangle, or any sided figure is the sum of the lengths of the sides:

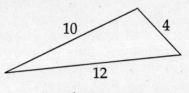

perimeter = 26

14. **perpendicular**—When two lines are perpendicular to each other, their intersection forms four 90-degree angles.

15. **pi (π)**—Pi (π) is 3.14; on the GRE CAT, $\pi = 3+$ is a close-enough approximation.

16. **Pythagorean theorem**—The Pythagorean theorem applies only to right triangles, which are triangles containing one 90-degree angle. The theorem states that in a right triangle, the square of the length of the hypotenuse (the longest side, the side opposite the right angle) equals the sum of the squares of the lengths of the two other sides. In other words, $c^2 = a^2 + b^2$ where c is the hypotenuse:

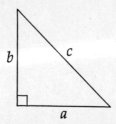

A common right triangle is the 3-4-5 right triangle, because $3^2 + 4^2 = 5^2$. You might see a multiple of that (such as 6-8-10) as well. The 5-12-13 right triangle also shows up occasionally.

17. **radius**—A line segment that joins the center of a circle with any point on its circumference. In this circle, the radius is 3:

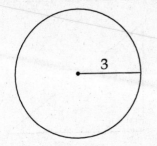

18. **rectangle**—A four-sided figure where the opposite sides are parallel and all angles are 90 degrees. The area of a rectangle is length times width ($A = lw$).

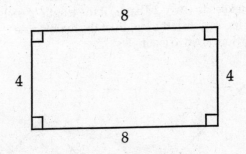

perimeter = 4 + 8 + 4 + 8 = 24

area = 8 × 4 = 32

19. **right angle**—Ninety-degree angles are also called right angles. A right angle on the GRE is identified by a little box at the intersection of the angle's sides:

20. **right triangle**—A right triangle is one in which one of the angles is a right angle—a 90-degree angle. The longest side of a right triangle—the side opposite the 90-degree angle—is called the hypotenuse:

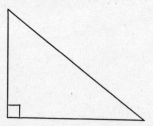

One special right triangle is the isosceles right triangle, or the 45:45:90 (those are its angle measures), in which the two non-hypotenuse sides are equal. The ratio between the length of either of them and that of the hypotenuse is 1:1: $\sqrt{2}$ That is, if the length of each short leg is x, then the length of the hypotenuse is $x\sqrt{2}$. Here are two examples:

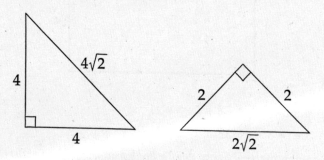

Another special right triangle is the 30:60:90 right triangle. Here's the ratio of its sides:

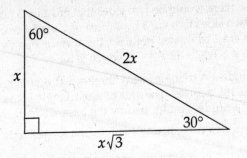

That is, if the shortest side is length x, then the hypotenuse is $2x$ and the remaining side is $x\sqrt{3}$. Here are two examples:

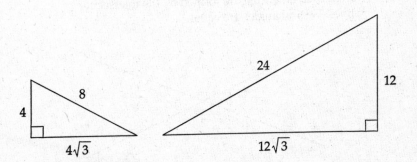

21. **slope**—In coordinate geometry, the equation of a line, or slope, is $y = mx + b$, where the x and the y are points on the line, b stands for the "y-intercept," or the point at which the line crosses the y-axis, and m is the actual slope of the line, or the change in y divided by the change in x. Note: Sometimes ETS uses an a instead of an m.

22. **square**—A square is a rectangle with four equal sides. The area is the length of any side times itself, which is to say, the length of any side squared ($A = s^2$).

23. **surface area**—The surface area of a rectangular box is equal to the sum of the areas of all of its sides. In other words, if you had a box whose dimensions were 2 by 3

by 4, there would be two sides that are 2 by 3 (area of 6), two sides that are 3 by 4 (area of 12), and two sides that are 2 by 4 (area of 8). So, the surface area would be $6 + 6 + 12 + 12 + 8 + 8$, which is 52.

24. **triangle**—A triangle is any three-sided figure, and contains 180 degrees. The area of any triangle is the height (or "altitude") multiplied by the base, divided by 2 ($A = \frac{1}{2} bh$). Also, in any triangle, the longest side is opposite the largest interior angle, the shortest side is opposite the smallest interior angle, and equal sides are opposite equal angles (see isosceles).

25. **vertical angles**—Vertical angles are the angles across from each other that are formed by the intersection of lines. Vertical angles are equal:

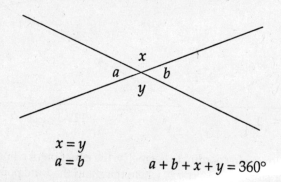

$$x = y$$
$$a = b$$
$$a + b + x + y = 360°$$

26. **volume**—The volume of a rectangular solid is $l \times w \times h$ (length times width times height). The volume of a circular cylinder is πr^2 (the area of the circle that forms the base) times the height (in other words, $\pi r^2 h$).

THE BIG TECHNIQUE: DRAW (OR REDRAW) IT YOURSELF

When ETS doesn't include a drawing with a geometry problem, it usually means that the drawing, if supplied, would make the answer obvious. In that case, you should just draw it yourself. Here's an example:

Column A	Column B
On a cube, the numberof faces that share anedge with any one face	The number of sides of a square

○ the quantity in Column A is always greater
○ the quantity in Column B is always greater
○ the quantities are always equal
○ different numbers would result in different answers

You're not going to settle for a picture-less geometry question, are you? Just make a quick sketch—something like this:

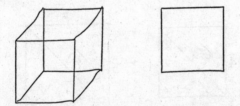

How many faces share an edge with any one face in our drawing of a cube? Looks like each face shares an edge with four other faces. The value of Column A, therefore, is 4. And how about Column B? A square has 4 sides. The values of the two columns are the same. The answer is (C). Isn't it helpful to see the picture?

Redraw

On quant comp questions, you may need to draw the figure once, eliminate two answer choices, then redraw the figure to try to disprove your first answer, in order to see if the answer is (D). Here's an example:

Column A
The length of the diagonal of a rectangle with perimeter 16

Column B
The length of the diagonal of a rectangle with perimeter 20

○ the quantity in Column A is always greater
○ the quantity in Column B is always greater
○ the quantities are always equal
○ different numbers would result in different answers

So, let's draw a rectangle with perimeter 16 and one with perimeter 20. It's easiest to make them squares (after all, a square is a rectangle with four equal sides).

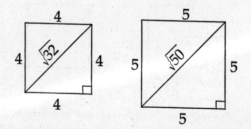

Remember, in quant comp, the answer is not what is in each column, but which is bigger. So just leave Column A as the square root of 32, and Column B as the square root of 50. Which is bigger? Column B. Eliminate choices (A) and (C). Now try to disprove that answer. Let's try to make the diagonal of the rectangle in Column A bigger. Think of "weird" numbers for the sides of the rectangle. How about sides of 1 and 7?

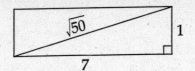

What's the diagonal of this rectangle? It's the square root of 50! So
we proved that answer choice (B) is wrong, and the answer must be (D).

STEP 7

BALLPARKING
(EQUATIONS I)

MATH SENTENCES?

Many GRE math problems involve words and letters, or variables, such as n, x, or y, in equations. It's time to learn how to deal with those. Before you learn the Big Technique for equations you need to warm up with some really basic algebra.

Solving for One Variable

Any equation with one variable can be solved by manipulating the equation. You get the variables on one side of the equation and the numbers on the other side. To do this, you can add, subtract, multiply, or divide both sides of the equation by the same number. Just remember that anything you do to one side of an equation, you have to do to the other side. Be sure to write down every step. Let's look at a simple example:

$$4x - 3 = 9$$

You can get rid of negatives by adding something to both sides of the equation, just as you can get rid of positives by subtracting something from both sides of the equation.

$$4x - 3 = 9$$
$$\underline{+3 \quad +3}$$
$$4x = 12$$

You may already see that $x = 3$. But don't forget to write down that last step. Divide both sides of the equation by 4.

$$\frac{4x}{4} = \frac{12}{4}$$

$$x = 3$$

MORE MATH VOCAB

1. **average**—The average (arithmetic mean) of a set of numbers is the sum, or total value, of all the numbers divided by the number of numbers in the set, or $A = \frac{T}{N}$. For example, the average of the set $\{1, 2, 3, 4, 5, 6, 7\}$ is the total of the numbers $(1 + 2 + 3 + 4 + 5 + 6 + 7$, or 28) divided by the number of numbers in the set (which is 7). Dividing 28 by 7 gives us 4. So, 4 is the average of the set. Now, say you were told that Sam's

average score for 4 math tests was 80 out of a possible 100. If his scores on 2 of the tests were 65 and 70, what is the lowest that either of his other scores could have been? First, find Sam's total score, using the formula:

$$80 = \frac{T}{4}$$
$$320 = T$$

Now, we know that two of his scores are 65 and 70. Let's call the other unknown test scores x and y:

$$65 + 70 + x + y = 320$$
$$135 + x + y = 320$$
$$x + y = 185$$

The question is, what is the lowest that either of his other scores could have been? Since the tests are only out of a possible 100, and the total of those two test scores is 185, he must have gotten an 85 and a 100. The lower score is 85, so that's the answer.

2. **F.O.I.L.**—F.O.I.L. stands for First, Outer, Inner, Last—the four steps of multiplication when you see two sets of parentheses. Here's an example:

$$(x + 4)(x + 3) = (x + 4)(x + 3)$$
$$= (x \times x) + (x \times 3) + (4 \times x) + (4 \times 3)$$
$$= x^2 + 3x + 4x + 12$$
$$= x^2 + 7x + 12$$

This also works in the opposite direction.

3. **factoring**—If you rewrite the expression $xy + xz$ as $x(y + z)$, you are said to be factoring the original expression. That is, you take the factor common to both terms of the original expression (x) and "pull it out." This gives you a new, "factored" version of the expression you began with. If you rewrite the

expression $x(y + z)$ as $xy + xz$, you are unfactoring the original expression.

4. **functions**—No, not real mathematical functions. On the GRE, a function is a funny-looking symbol that stands for an operation. For example, say you're told that $m @ n$ is equal to $\frac{m + n}{n - 1}$. What's the value of 4 @ 6? Just follow directions: $\frac{4 + 6}{6 - 1}$, or $\frac{10}{5}$, or 2. Don't worry that "@" isn't a real mathematical operation; it could have been a "#" or a "&," or any other symbol. The point is, just do what they tell you to do.

5. **inequalities**—Here are the symbols you need to know: $\neq$ means not equal to; $>$ means greater than; $<$ means less than; $\geq$ means greater than or equal to; $\leq$ means less than or equal to. You can manipulate any inequality in the same way you can an equation, with one important difference. For example:

$$10 - 5x > 0$$

You can solve this by subtracting 10 from both sides of the equation, and ending up with $-5x > -10$. Now you have to divide both sides by -5:

$$-5x / -5 > -10 / -5$$

which means you have to flip the sign:

$$x < 2$$

6. **percent**—Percent means "per 100" or "out of 100" or "divided by 100." If your friend finds a dollar and gives you 50 cents, your friend has given you 50 cents out of 100, or $\frac{50}{100}$ of a dollar, or 50 percent of a dollar.

When you have to find exact percentages it's much easier if you know how to translate word problems, which lets you express them as equations. Here's a translation "dictionary":

Word	Translates to
percent	/100 (example: 40 percent translates to $\frac{40}{100}$)
is	=
of	×
what any variable	(x, k, b)
what percent	$\frac{x}{100}$

What is 30 percent of 200?

First translate it, using the "dictionary" above:

$$x = \frac{30}{100} \times 200$$

Now reduce that 100 and 200, and solve for the variable, like this:

$$x = 30 \times 2$$
$$x = 60$$

So, 30 percent of 200 is 60.

7. **percent increase/decrease**—To find a percentage increase or decrease, first find the amount of increase or decrease, then put it over the starting point number, and multiply it by $\frac{x}{100}$. In other words:

Percent change $= \frac{x}{100} \times$ original number (starting point)

For example, if you had to find the percent decrease from 4 to 3, first figure out what the actual decrease is.

The decrease from 4 to 3 is 1. So, $1 = \frac{x}{100} \times 4$, since 4 is the original number. Now solve for x:

$$1 = \frac{4x}{100}$$

$$1 = \frac{x}{25}$$

$$25 = x$$

So, the percent decrease from 4 to 3 is 25 percent.

8. **proportion**—A proportion takes a given relationship, or ratio, and projects it onto a larger or smaller scale. For example, if 10 baskets contain a total of 50 eggs, how many eggs would 7 baskets contain? Set up a proportion of $\frac{\text{baskets}}{\text{eggs}} = \frac{10}{50} = \frac{7}{x}$. Because you can treat ratios exactly like fractions, you can find the missing element by cross-multiplying:

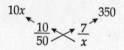

$$10x = 350$$

$$x = 35$$

Note that we could have made our cross-multiplication simpler by reducing $\frac{10}{50}$ to $\frac{1}{5}$ before cross-multiplying.

9. **quadratic equations**—Three equations that sometimes show up on the GRE. Here they are, in their factored and unfactored forms:

Factored form		Unfactored form
$x^2 - y^2$	=	$(x + y)(x - y)$
$(x + y)^2$	=	$x^2 + 2xy + y^2$
$(x - y)^2$	=	$x^2 - 2xy + y^2$

10. **ratio**—Ratios, like fractions, percentages, and decimals, are just another way of representing division. A ratio is an abstract relationship that is always reduced. If there were 14 red marbles and 16 blue marbles in a bowl, the ratio of red to blue marbles in the bowl would be 7:8 (which could also be written as $\frac{7}{8}$). Now, say you were told that at a camp, the ratio of the girls to boys is 5:3. If the camp's total enrollment is 160, how many of the children are boys? A ratio of 5:3 doesn't mean literally 5 girls and 3 boys. It means 8 total parts (because $5 + 3 = 8$). To find out how many children are in each "part," we divide the total enrollment by the number of "parts." Dividing 160 by 8 gives us 20. That means each part is 20 children. Three of the parts are boys, which means there are 3×20, or 60 boys.

11. **simultaneous equations**—Two algebraic equations that include the same variables. For example, what if you were told that $5x + 4y = 6$ and $4x + 3y = 5$, and asked what $x + y$ equals? To solve a set of simultaneous equations, you can usually either add them together or subtract one from the other (just remember when you subtract that everything you're subtracting needs to be made negative). Here's what we get when we add them:

$$5x + 4y = 6$$
$$\underline{+\ 4x + 3y = 5}$$
$$9x + 7y = 11$$

A dead end. So let's try subtraction:

$$5x + 4y = 6$$
$$\underline{-\ 4x - 3y = -5}$$
$$x + y = 1$$

Eureka. The value of the expression $(x + y)$ is exactly what we're looking for.

THE BIG TECHNIQUE: BALLPARKING

Say you were asked to find 30 percent of 50. Don't do any math yet. Now let's say that you glance at the answer choices and you see these:

○ 5
○ 15
○ 30
○ 80
○ 150

Think about it. Whatever 30 percent of 50 is, it must be less than 50, right? So any answer choice greater than 50 can't be right. That means you should eliminate both 80 and 150 right off the bat, without doing any math. You can also eliminate 30, if you think about it. Half, or 50 percent, of 50 is 25, so 30 percent must be less than 25. Congratulations, you've just eliminated three out of five answer choices without doing any math.

What we've just done is known as Ballparking. Ballparking will help you eliminate answer choices and increase your odds of zeroing in on ETS' answer. Remember to eliminate any answer choice that is "out of the ballpark" by crossing them off on your scratch paper (remember, you'll be writing down A, B, C, D, E for each question).

Charts

Ballparking will also help you on the few chart questions that every GRE math section will have. You should Ballpark whenever you see the word "approximately" in a question, whenever the answer choices are far apart in value, and whenever you start to answer a question and you justifiably say to yourself, "This is going to take a lot of calculation!"

To help you Ballpark, here are a few percents and their fractional equivalents:

$$1\% = \frac{1}{100}$$

$$50\% = \frac{1}{2}$$

$$60\% = \frac{3}{5}$$

$$10\% = \frac{1}{10}$$

$$66\frac{2}{3}\% = \frac{2}{3}$$

$$20\% = \frac{1}{5}$$

$$75\% = \frac{3}{4}$$

$$25\% = \frac{1}{4}$$

$$80\% = \frac{4}{5}$$

$$33\frac{1}{3}\% = \frac{1}{3}$$

$$100\% = \frac{1}{1}$$

$$40\% = \frac{2}{5}$$

$$200\% = \frac{2}{1}$$

If, on a chart question, you were asked to find 9.6 percent of 21.4, you could Ballpark by using 10 percent as a "friendlier" percentage and 20 as a "friendlier" number. Ten percent of 20 is 2. That's all you need to do to answer most chart questions.

Let's try out Ballparking on a real chart. Keep in mind that while friends give you charts to display the information they want you to see and to make that information easier to understand, ETS constructs charts to *hide* the information you need to know and to make that information *hard* to understand. So read all titles and small print, to make sure you understand what the charts are conveying.

Nationwide survey of ice cream preferences in 1975 and in 1985, by flavor.

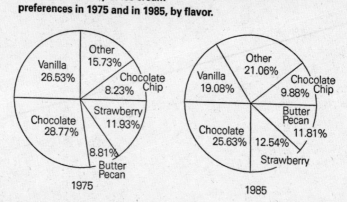

1975

1985

Looking over these charts, we notice that they are for 1975 and 1985, and that all we know are percentages. There are no total numbers for the survey, and since the percentages are pretty "ugly," we can anticipate doing a lot of Ballparking to answer the questions. Let's try one:

> To the nearest one percent, what percentage decrease in popularity occurred for chocolate from 1975 to 1985?
>
> ○ 9%
> ○ 10%
> ○ 11%
> ○ 89%
> ○ 90%

First, we need to find the difference between 28.77 (the 1975 figure) and 25.63 (the 1985 figure). The difference is 3.14. Second, notice that ETS has asked for an approximate answer ("to the nearest one percent") which is screaming "Ballpark!" Could 3.14 really be 89 or 90 percent of 28.77? No way; it's closer to the neighborhood of 10 percent. Eliminate choices (D) and (E). Is it exactly 10 percent? No; that means choice B is out. Is it more or less than 10 percent? It's more—exactly 10 percent would be 2.877, and 3.14 is more than 2.877. That means the answer is (C).

Let's try another one:

> In 1985, if 20 percent of the "other" category is lemon flavor, and 4,212 people surveyed preferred lemon, then how many people were surveyed?
>
> ○ 1,000
> ○ 10,000
> ○ 42,120
> ○ 100,000
> ○ 1,000,000

The first piece of information we have is a percentage of a percentage. The percentage of people who preferred lemon in 1985 is equal to 20 percent of 21.06 percent. Make sure you see that before we go on. Now notice that the numbers in the answer choices are very widely separated—they aren't consecutive integers. If we can just get in the Ballpark, the answer will be obvious.

Rather than try to use 21.06 percent, we'll call it 20 percent. And rather than use 4,212, we'll use 4,000. The question is now: "20 percent of 20 percent of *what* is 4,000?" So, using translation, your equation looks like this:

$$\frac{20}{100} \times \frac{20}{100} \times x = 4,000$$

Do a little reducing.

$$\frac{1}{5} \times \frac{1}{5} \times x = 4,000$$

$$\frac{1}{25} \times x = 4,000$$

$$x = 100,000$$

That's (D). One more question:

> Which of the following statements can be deduced from the pie graphs?
>
> I. Both the butter pecan and vanilla percentages increased by more than 33 percent between 1975 and 1985.
>
> II. A higher percentage of people chose butter pecan and strawberry in 1975 than chose butter pecan and chocolate chip in 1985.
>
> III. The total share of vanilla, chocolate, and strawberry decreased by less than 20 percent from 1975 to 1985.
>
> ○ I only
> ○ II only
> ○ III only
> ○ II and III
> ○ I, II, and III

First, check out Statement I. Did the butter pecan percentage increase by more than 33 percent (one-third)? It increased from 8.81 to 11.81. That's a 3-point increase. Is 3 more than one-third of 8.81? Yes. Okay so far. Now check vanilla. Vanilla went from 26.53 to 19.08. That's a decrease, not an increase. Statement I isn't true. We can eliminate any choice that has Roman Numeral I in it—(A) and (E). Now let's try Statement II. What's the combined percentage for butter pecan and strawberry in 1975? It's 8.81 plus 11.93, or 20.74. What's the combined percentage for butter pecan and chocolate chip in 1985? It's 11.81 plus 9.88, or 21.69. Statement II is false. We can eliminate choices (B) and (D). No need to check the remaining statement: We're left with (C).

STEP 8

PLUGGING IN
(EQUATIONS II)

In the last chapter we actually did some simple algebra. It wasn't so bad, was it? But what if you saw something like this?

> Kyle has four fewer toys than Scott, but seven more toys than Jody. If Kyle has k toys, then how many toys do Scott and Jody have together?

- ○ $2k + 11$
- ○ $2k + 7$
- ○ $2k + 3$
- ○ $2k - 3$
- ○ $2k - 11$

Tempted to start setting up an equation for algebra? Don't. Numbers are much easier to work with in math than letters, or variables, are. Wouldn't this question be a whole lot easier if you knew what k was?

THE BIG TECHNIQUE: PLUGGING IN

Let's just take control and decide what k is. Go on—it's okay. "Plug In" a number for k. Make it a nice round number, like 10. So now the question reads:

> Kyle has four fewer toys than Scott, but seven more toys than Jody. If Kyle has 10 toys, then how many toys do Scott and Jody have together?

Much better, right? Kyle has 10 toys, and he also has four fewer than Scott, so how many does Scott have? Fourteen. Kyle also has seven more toys than Jody, so how many does Jody have? She must have three. And what was the actual question? How many toys do Scott and Jody have together? 14 + 3, or 17. Bingo. The answer to the question is 17. Now let's bring back the answer choices.

- ○ $2k + 11$
- ○ $2k + 7$
- ○ $2k + 3$
- ○ $2k - 3$
- ○ $2k - 11$

Oh no, there's no 17 here! Oh yes there is. We made $k = 10$, remember? Let's follow it through. Every time you see a k, make it a 10, like this:

(A) $2(10) + 11$

(B) $2(10) + 7$

(C) $2(10) + 3$

(D) $2(10) - 3$

(E) $2(10) - 11$

Now let's work them out:

(A) $2(10) + 11 = 20 + 11 = 31$

(B) $2(10) + 7 = 20 + 7 = 27$

(C) $2(10) + 3 = 20 + 3 = 23$

(D) $2(10) - 3 = 20 - 3 = 17$

(E) $2(10) - 11 = 20 - 11 = 9$

Is there a 17 in the answer choices now? Yup, choice (D).

Hold on, you're thinking. This can't be. We picked 10 for a reason, right? Nope. In fact, any number will work, and give us the same answer. It has to. Plugging In makes word problems much less abstract, and much easier to solve.

Here's what we just did, and what you should always do when you see variables in a question or in answer choices:

Step 1: Pick a number for each variable in the problem and *write it down* on your scratch paper.

Step 2: Solve the problem using your numbers, *write your numerical answer and circle it*; that's your "target answer."

Step 3: *Write down the answer choices* and plug your number in for each one to see which one of them equals the solution you found in step 2.

Even if you think you can do the algebra, Plug In instead. Why? Because if you do the algebra and you're wrong, you won't know it because one of ETS' wrong answers will be there waiting for you— that's how they come up with their wrong answers, by figuring out every mistake a tester could make. But if you Plug In, and you're wrong, you won't get an answer, and you'll know you're wrong, forcing you to try again. Plugging In is foolproof. Algebra isn't.

Let's try another one:

If $3a + 4b = 4a - 3b$, then $a =$

○ $-b$

○ $\frac{3b}{4}$

○ b

○ $6b$

○ $7b$

Two variables? No problem. We need to know what a is. If we knew what b was, it would be much easier to solve for a. Let's take control and decide what b is. We'll make it 5. Plug In 5 every time you see b in the question, so this

$$3a + 4b = 4a - 3b$$

becomes this

$$3a + 4(5) = 4a - 3(5)$$

or this

$$3a + 20 = 4a - 15$$

Much easier, right? Now let's solve for a:

$$3a + 20 = 4a - 15$$
$$\underline{ + 15 + 15}$$
$$3a + 35 = 4a$$
$$\underline{-3a - 3a}$$
$$35 = a$$

Okay, now let's bring in the answer choices:

○ $-b$

○ $\frac{3b}{4}$

○ b

○ $6b$

○ $7b$

Oh no, there's no 35 here! Yes there is. Remember, we made $b = 5$. We just have to carry it through. Rewrite the answer choices, Plugging In 5 every time you see b:

(A) $-(5)$

(B) $\dfrac{3(5)}{4} = \dfrac{15}{4}$

(C) 5

(D) $6(5) = 30$

(E) $7(5) = 35$

Now do you see 35 in the answer choices? Yup, choice (E).

You should *never* try to solve problems like these by "solving for x" or "solving for y." Plugging In is much easier and faster, and you'll be less likely to make careless mistakes.

Good Numbers Make Life Easier

You can Plug In any numbers you like, as long as they're consistent with any restrictions stated in the problem. But you'll find the answer faster if you use easy numbers.

What makes a number easy? That depends on the problem. In many cases, smaller numbers are easier to work with than larger numbers. You should avoid Plugging In numbers that are used in the question or the answer choices. Also avoid Plugging In 0 and 1 in these situations; there's a time and a place for them, because they have special properties. You'll learn more about that later.

Small numbers aren't always best. In a problem involving percentages, for example, 10 and 100 are good numbers to use. In a problem involving minutes or seconds, 60 may be the easiest number to Plug In. Take a look:

> The average test score earned by a group of students is 80. If 40 percent of the students have an average score of 70, what is the average score of the remaining 60 percent?
>
> ○ $70\frac{1}{3}$
> ○ 80
> ○ $86\frac{2}{3}$
> ○ 90
> ○ 95

We don't have variables in the answer choices in this case, but there is an important piece of information missing from this problem: the number of students in the group. Just plug one in! Because we're dealing with percentages, 10 is an easy number to work with. So we'll assume that our group contains 10 students. Four of those 10 (40 percent of 10) students have an average score of 70; we're supposed to determine the average score of the remaining 6.

The first thing we need to do (now that we've turned it back into an easy averaging problem) is to find the total. If the average score of 10 students is 80, what's their total score? It's 800. Four of the students have an average score of 70, which means that their total score is 280. What's the total score of the remaining 6 students? It's 800 − 280, or 520. What's their average score (which is what we're looking for)? It's 520 ÷ 6, or $86\frac{2}{3}$. That's (C).

Plugging In The Answer Choices

Take a look at this:

> Two positive integers, x and y, have a difference of 15. If the smaller integer, y, is $\frac{5}{8}$ of x, then what is the value of y?
>
> ○ 40
> ○ 25
> ○ 20
> ○ 15
> ○ 10

We don't have variables in the answer choices, but we've got them in the question. Since they're asking for the value of one of the variables, let's just Plug In the answers. After all, one of them has to be right. Just remember to write down all the answer choices on your scratch paper so you can cross them out as you go.

When you Plug In the answer choices, it's usually a good idea to start in the middle and work your way out. Why? Because GRE answer choices are almost always arranged in order of size. You may be able to tell not only that a particular choice is incorrect, but also that it is too big or too small. Sometimes you can eliminate three choices just by trying one. So let's make $y = 20$, which is choice (C). According to the second sentence of the problem, y is $\frac{5}{8}$ of x; in other words, 20 is $\frac{5}{8}$ of x.

Let's rewrite that (a little translation):

$$20 = \frac{5}{8}x$$

Multiply both sides by the reciprocal of $\frac{5}{8}$, which is $\frac{8}{5}$:

$$\left(\frac{8}{5}\right)(20) = \left(\frac{8}{5}\right)\left(\frac{5}{8}\right)x$$

$$32 = x$$

The rest of the problem says that the difference between x and y is 15. Is the difference between 20 and 32 equal to 15? Nope, it's 12. Let's try again, with a bigger number: choice (B), 25. y is $\frac{5}{8}$ of x; in other words, 25 is $\frac{5}{8}$ of x. Let's rewrite that:

$$25 = \frac{5}{8}x$$

Multiply both sides by the reciprocal of $\frac{5}{8}$, which is $\frac{8}{5}$:

$$\left(\frac{8}{5}\right)(25) = \left(\frac{8}{5}\right)\left(\frac{5}{8}\right)x$$

$$40 = x$$

The rest of the problem says that the difference between x and y is 15. Is the difference between 25 and 40 equal to 15? Yes it is. The answer is (B). Why do more work than we have to, when we can just Plug In the answer choices?

Plugging In on "Must Be" Problems

Sometimes you'll be asked which answer choice "must be true." These "algebraic reasoning" problems are much easier to solve by Plugging In than by "reasoning." On these, you will have to Plug In more than once in order to find the answer. Here's an example:

The positive difference between the squares of any two consecutive integers must be

○ the square of an integer
○ a multiple of 5
○ an even integer
○ an odd number
○ a prime number

The words "must be" in the question (it also might have said "must always be") tell us that all we need to find in order to eliminate a choice is a single instance in which it doesn't work. So let's start by picking two consecutive integers and squaring them. It doesn't matter which consecutive integers we choose. How about 2 and 3? Squaring 2 and 3 gives us 4 and 9. The positive difference between them (9 – 4, as opposed to 4 – 9) is 5. Now look at the choices:

(A) Is 5 the square of an integer? No. Eliminate.

(B) Is 5 a multiple of 5? Yes. A possibility.

(C) Is 5 an even integer? No. Eliminate.

(D) Is 5 an odd integer? Yes. A possibility.

(E) Is 5 a prime number? Yes. A possibility.

We've eliminated choices (A) and (C). That's good. It means that with very little effort we've boosted our guessing odds to 1 in 3. But we can do better than that. Let's pick two more consecutive integers. How about 0 and 1? The squares of 0 and 1 are 0 and 1. The positive difference between them is 1. Now look at the remaining choices:

(B) Is 1 a multiple of 5? No. Eliminate.

(D) Is 1 an odd integer? Yes. A possibility.

(E) Is 1 a prime number? No. Eliminate. The answer is (D).

Notice that on the second round of elimination we Plugged In "weird" numbers that we usually avoid. That's how we found what would always be true. That leads us to . . .

Plugging In on Quant Comp

Because answer choice (D) is always an option on quant comps, you always have to make sure it isn't the answer. So Plugging In on quant comp is just like it is on "must be" problems—you have to do it twice. On quant comps, it's not enough to determine whether one quantity is sometimes greater than, less than, or equal to the other; you have to determine whether it *always* is. If different numbers lead to different answers, then the answer is choice (D). Let's try it:

Column A	Column B
	$\dfrac{1}{b}$
b	

○ the quantity in Column A is always greater

○ the quantity in Column B is always greater

○ the quantities are always equal

○ different numbers would result in different answers

Let's start by Plugging In a nice, easy number for b, like 10. That gives us 10 in Column A and $\dfrac{1}{10}$ in Column B. So the answer's (A), right?

Not so fast. We always have to Plug In twice on quant comps. Our first round gave us (A), which really only means that the answer *cannot* be (B) or (C). Choice (D) is still in the running. Our second round of plugging in should involve a "weird" number, a number that we would try to avoid the first time around, something that might shake things up a bit. How about 1? If $b = 1$, we get 1 in Column A and 1 in Column B. That's (C). But we've already gotten rid of (C). Since we Plugged In twice, and got different answers each time, the answer must be (D) for "different."

Here's the procedure:

Step 1: Write A, B, C, D, on your scratch paper.

Step 2: Plug In "normal" numbers like 2, 3, 5, or 10.

Step 3: Which column is bigger? Cross out the two choices that you've proved are wrong. Suppose the numbers you Plugged In at first made Column A bigger. Which answer choices cannot be correct? (B) and (C). Cross them out! (A) and (D) are still possible choices.

Step 4: Now *try* to get a different answer by Plugging In weird numbers such as 0, 1, negatives, fractions, or really big numbers. If you get a different result, the answer is (D). If you don't, it's whatever you keep getting.

Why are 0, 1, negatives, fractions, or really big numbers considered "weird" numbers? Because they do weird things. For example:

- 0 times any number is 0

- 1 times any number is the number

- 0^2 is 0

- 1^2 is 1

- Any number to the first power is itself

- Fractions get smaller as you raise them to powers

- A negative number squared is positive

- Really big numbers (100, 1,000) can make a really big difference in your answer

What About Geometry?

On geometry problems, you can Plug In values for angles or lengths if the values you Plug In don't contradict either the wording of the problem or the laws of geometry (you can't let the interior angles of a triangle add up to anything but 180, for instance). For example:

Column A   Column B

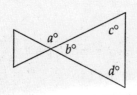

$c + d$ a

- ○ the quantity in Column A is always greater
- ○ the quantity in Column B is always greater
- ○ the quantities are always equal
- ○ different numbers would result in different answers

Start with the triangle containing angles b, c, and d. Whatever those angles might be separately, together they must add up to 180 degrees. Let's Plug In three numbers that add up to 180, say, $b = 50$, $c = 60$, $d = 70$. Now we can figure out what a would have to be with those numbers; it's on the same line as b, and a straight line has 180 degrees. So, if b is 50, a must be 130.

Column A is $60 + 70$, or 130. Column B is 130. The answer is (C).

Note: In most cases, there's no need to plug in twice on geometry quant comp, since most weird numbers don't work in GRE geometry. (You can't have a negative length!)

BREAK IT DOWN
(ARGUMENTS)

What's an Argument?

A GRE argument is not the kind of disagreement you have with a sibling. It's a paragraph that states a *conclusion* (a claim or point) with the support of *premises* (reasons or evidence). For example, in the argument "Vote for me because I will not raise taxes," the conclusion (the thing the author wants you to know or do) is "Vote for me . . . " and the premise, or the reason you should do it, is ". . . because I will not raise taxes."

On the GRE the argument is followed by a question about the content of the argument and five answer choices. Let's look at an example:

> Some people in the publishing business, concerned about the expense of publishing scholarly works and other esoteric titles, have suggested that research be done to determine in advance the probability of sales before such books are published. Opponents of this proposal argue that such books should be published in the name of education and enlightenment, and, in any case, that it is impossible to predict sales of any kind of literature in advance, because of unforeseen trends and changes in public tastes.
>
> Which of the following best states the opponents' main point?
>
> ○ Publishing scholarly works whose sales are indeterminable is morally superior to publishing books that will appeal to current public tastes.
>
> ○ In an ideal world, all books would be published, regardless of sales; however, this would not be possible economically.
>
> ○ Since there is no absolutely certain method for determining in advance the potential sales and public interest in a book, a publisher cannot and should not make publishing

decisions as if there were such a
method.

○ It is more vital to the public interest
to publish books that are scholarly
and esoteric than to publish books
that sell well.

○ It is impossible to determine the
popularity of some books.

The biggest mistake testers make on arguments is reading the
paragraph quickly and going right to the answers.

THE BIG TECHNIQUE: BREAK IT DOWN

You have to *break down* the argument so you know what it's about,
and then use POE to *break down* the answer choices. How do you
break down the argument? The first thing you do is read the
question—not the argument, the actual question.

Why read the question first? The question tells you what to look
for in the passage and how to approach it. Let's look at the question
from that argument again:

> Which of the following best states the
> opponents' main point?

Now we know when we go to the argument that we should focus
on the opponents' opinion. Now let's read the argument:

> Some people in the publishing busi-
> ness, concerned about the expense of
> publishing scholarly works and other
> esoteric titles, have suggested that
> research be done to determine in
> advance the probability of sales before
> such books are published. Opponents
> of this proposal argue that such books
> should be published in the name of
> education and enlightenment, and, in
> any case, that it is impossible to predict
> sales of any kind of literature in
> advance, because of unforeseen trends
> and changes in public tastes.

Okay, let's break it down: Take a minute to restate the argument *in your own words*. "Some people are only worried about book sales. Opponents say education and enlightenment are more important than sales, and you can't really predict literature sales in advance." That's it. Don't get fancy, just break it down for yourself. Now, the question asked for a restatement of the opponents' main point, something like "education and enlightenment are more important than sales, and you can't really predict literature sales in advance."

Now, onto POE, your new religion. Let's break down those answer choices, looking for the closest thing to "education and enlightenment are more important than sales, and you can't really predict literature sales in advance." Always read all five answer choices, and remember, the key to doing well on arguments is the same as everywhere else on the test: Narrow your thinking. All you know about the topic is what you've been told in the argument. Nothing else!

○ Publishing scholarly works whose sales are indeterminable is morally superior to publishing books that will appeal to current public tastes.

"Morally superior?"

○ In an ideal world, all books would be published, regardless of sales; however, this would not be possible economically.

An "ideal world?"

○ Since there is no absolutely certain method for determining in advance the potential sales and public interest in a book, a publisher cannot and should not make publishing decisions as if there were such a method.

In other words, "you can't really predict literature sales in advance." Sounds pretty good. Hold onto this one, but *always* read all five answer choices.

○ It is more vital to the public interest to publish books that are scholarly and esoteric than to publish books that sell well.

"Vital to the public interest?"

○ It is impossible to determine the popularity of some books.

"Impossible?" Sounds pretty extreme.

So, the best answer is (C), if only because the other four are worse. That's how it is with arguments. You're finding the "best" answer by eliminating the bad ones. But maybe you're not sure how we got rid of those other choices. Notice that we critiqued those wrong choices by questioning the language used in them. For example, we didn't like (A) because there was nothing in the argument about "moral superiority." We didn't like (B) because there was nothing in the argument about an "ideal world." We didn't like (D) because there's nothing in the argument about what's "vital to the public interest." Public interest in a certain book, maybe. The "public interest" as a whole? No. We didn't like (E) because it's pretty extreme to say it's "impossible" to determine the popularity of some books. But we liked (C) because there *is* something in the argument about not being able to predict potential sales.

Scope

What choices (A), (B), and (D) all have in common is that they mention information that is not in the *scope* of the argument. Scope is a huge part of your answer choice breakdown process. The most important consideration when using POE is whether an answer choice goes outside the scope of the argument. The scope of an argument is defined very narrowly; it's restricted by the conclusion and premises as stated in the passage.

If an answer choice goes beyond the issues of the argument, then it's *outside the scope* and you *must* eliminate it! If you have to make a case for the answer choice ("Well, if you look at it this way . . .") it's outside the scope. Remember that all you know about the topic is what you've been told in the passage! Don't consider whatever outside knowledge or opinions you may have regarding the issues in the argument.

Extreme Wording

The problem with choice (E) was that it was extreme. The best answer to many questions (we'll tell you about the exceptions) will use indisputable, rather than extreme, language. Indisputable (soft) answer choices tend to use words like *can, may, might, often, some,* etc. Extreme answer choices tend to use words like *all, always, totally, must, no, only,* or *the best, the first.* When two answer choices seem very similar, look for these differences in wording.

Use More Than One Round of Elimination

The first time you break down the answer choices, you should eliminate those answers that you know for sure are out of the scope. If you're not sure what an answer choice means (don't be ashamed to admit it!) don't eliminate it at first. When you're down to two or three choices, on the second round of elimination, you'll have to look more closely at the choices left. Focus on what makes an answer wrong, word by word. You don't have to understand why the best answer is right, only why the other four choices can't be the correct choice.

Ready to Try Again?

Here's another one. We'll give it to you in the order that you should read it, with the question first:

> Which of the following can be inferred from the passage above?

On the GRE, "inferred" means something different than what it means in real life. On the GRE, it means "Which one of these answer choices is *known to be true* based on the information in the argument?" So, if you see the words "inference," "inferred," "implied," "which of the following must also be true," or "most properly be drawn," you know your job is to find the answer that you know is true. It doesn't have to be the conclusion of the argument, it just has to be true, according to the argument. Now, here's the argument:

> A New York hospital recently performed a ten-week weight-loss experiment involving men and women. Participants lost an average of twenty-five pounds. Male participants lost an average of forty pounds, while female participants lost an average of twenty pounds. Doctors connected with the study attributed the difference to the greater initial starting weights of the male participants.

Summarize it quickly in your own words: "In a weight-loss experiment, men lost more weight than women, possibly because of the men's higher initial starting weights." That's it. Now let's break down the answers. Because this is an inference question, after you read each answer choice, ask yourself, "Do I *know* this?"

○ No female participant had a starting weight greater than that of any of the male participants.

Do we know that "no" female participant had a starting weight greater than that of "any" male? The words "no" and "any" are too extreme. Eliminate this one.

○ Everyone who participated in the study lost weight.

Do we know that "everyone" lost weight? No. We have only average weight-loss figures. Eliminate it.

○ The study included more female than male participants.

You may think initially that we don't know this from the information we've been given. But this is known to be true. How? The males lost an average of forty pounds; the females lost an average of twenty pounds. If there had been exactly as many males as females in the study, the average weight loss for the group would have been thirty pounds—not the twenty-five pounds given in the passage. To account for the twenty-five-pound average, there had to be more females than males. The lower results for the females pulled down the group average. Keep it.

○ Some of the participants did not lose weight.

Do we know this? It could be true, but we don't know. We have only average weight-loss figures. Eliminate it.

○ The average starting weight of the male participants was twice that of the female participants.

Do we know that the males weighed exactly "twice" as much as the females? We don't know this. Eliminate it. The best answer is choice (C). Let's try again. Here's another argument, question first:

Which of the following is an assumption of the argument above?

The question asks us to find an *assumption*, which is an unstated reason or premise that strengthens or helps the conclusion. So, read the argument, keeping in mind that we need to know what the conclusion is so we can strengthen it.

> Most scientists agree that life requires a planetary body. If so, the possibility of extraterrestrial life in our galaxy has increased dramatically. Astronomers have just discovered an enormous number of possible planetary systems in conjunction with nearby stars. There may be millions or even billions of planets in our galaxy alone.

Quick summary breakdown: "The possibility of extraterrestrial life in our galaxy has increased dramatically." Why? Because "astronomers have just discovered an enormous number of possible planetary systems in conjunction with nearby stars." What's being assumed? That what's true of nearby stars is true of our galaxy. The conclusion is a generalization made from a sample of evidence. So the assumption has to be that the sample is representative. Now let's break down the answer choices, asking, "Does this help?"

○ There is an enormous number of planets in our galaxy.

Does this strengthen the conclusion that the possibility of extraterrestrial life in our galaxy has increased dramatically? Just because there are a lot of planets? It doesn't really help. Eliminate.

○ Life will soon be discovered in nearby planetary systems.

Really? You sure about that? Can you prove it?

○ Extraterrestrial life does not necessarily require earth-like conditions to exist.

Other conditions for life to exist, aside from the requirement of a planetary body, are outside the scope of this argument. Eliminate.

○ We will recognize extraterrestrial life when we encounter it.

And this is related to the conclusion . . . . how? It isn't.

○ Nearby stars are representative of
our galaxy as a whole.

This has to be the answer. The conclusion about the possibility of
extraterrestrial life in our galaxy is based on observations of nearby
stars. If that's true, then what is true of nearby stars must be true of the
galaxy as a whole. This helps the argument, which means it could be
used as a premise.

Anything that could be used as a premise is an assumption. You
can use the same basic techniques when you're asked to strengthen an
argument, but there's one difference: Don't be afraid to pick answers
with more extreme language when you're strengthening or weakening
an argument. Speaking of which, here we go again, question first:

Which of the following, if true, would
most strongly weaken the argument
above?

Here we're being asked to weaken the argument, which we do by
attacking the reasons, evidence, or premises of the argument, not just
by contradicting the conclusion. Anytime we're asked to "weaken,"
"challenge," "critique," "cast the most doubt," or anything else negative, our job is to attack. Here's the argument:

An analysis of factory productivity has
shown that productivity decreases as
the amount of factory output increases.
Since new employees are often hired
when a factory expects an increase in
output, the productivity drop can be
attributed to the unfamiliarity these new
employees have with the factory's operations.

Quick summary breakdown: "As output goes up, productivity
goes down." The reason, or premise, is that the high output brings
new employees, who are unfamiliar with operations. To attack this, we
need to show that the supposed premise, about the new employees, is
not valid. Let's break down the answer choices:

○ Many of the employees hired to produce the increased outputs are no longer employed after three months.

We don't care how long they're there. The question is, are they responsible for the decreased productivity *while* they're there? Eliminate.

○ The analysis only considered factories which forecast increased output rather than those that actually experienced an increase in output.

This is irrelevant. The question is, were new employees responsible for the decreased productivity from whichever factories participated? Eliminate.

○ Productivity is lower in factories than in any other type of commercial activity.

Other types of commercial activity are outside the scope. We only care about factories. Eliminate.

○ The productivity of employees who had been at the factory for more than ten years also declines during periods of increased output.

Ahh, so it's not the new employees who are responsible for the decrease in productivity. It's the folks who have been there for more than ten years. Bingo!

○ Factories must provide training to all new employees prior to allowing them onto the factory floor.

That may be true, but that doesn't mean that the new employees are not still responsible for decreased productivity. Even with training, they could still be slower than the older employees. The best answer is (D).

Here's another one, question first:

The two underlined statements above serve which of the following functions?

We now know to pay special attention to any portions of the argument that are underlined. Here's the argument:

> Although I just had service performed on my car's engine, it is still not running well. During the service, the timing belt was replaced, and the fuel filter was checked and found to be sound. <u>So the problem with the engine cannot be the timing belt or fuel filter.</u> Most cars of the same model and year as mine have experienced either timing belt slippage or water pump failure. <u>Therefore, the problem with my engine must be a failing water pump.</u>

Let's break it down: His car had engine service, but it didn't help. So the problem must not have been the stuff that was fixed (including the timing belt). Similar cars have either the timing belt problem or a water pump problem. Thus, his problem must be with the water pump. The first underlined portion is like a semiconclusion; it's the conclusion of everything up till that point. The second underlined portion is the conclusion of the whole argument. Here are the answers; let's POE 'em:

> ⭘ The first statement provides context for the argument, and the second statement serves as a premise supporting the main conclusion.

The second statement is the main conclusion of the argument, so eliminate this choice.

> ⭘ The first statement is a premise that supports an intermediate conclusion, and the second statement is the main conclusion of the argument.

That first underlined statement looks like an opinion, not a fact, and therefore not a premise. Eliminate.

○ The first statement is an intermedi-
ate conclusion that is refuted by the
main conclusion, and the second
statement is the main conclusion of
the argument.

The first statement is not refuted by the conclusion. Eliminate.

○ The first statement is an intermedi-
ate conclusion that supports the
main conclusion, and the second
statement is the main conclusion of
the argument.

Looks good, because the first statement looks like a conclusion of
some sort, and it definitely supports the main conclusion, and the second statement is definitely the main conclusion.

○ The first statement is the main conclusion of the argument, and the
second statement is an intermedi-
ate conclusion that supports the
main conclusion.

The second statement is the main conclusion of the argument, so
eliminate this answer choice. (D) is the best answer.

STEP 10

DRAW A DIAGRAM
(GAMES)

What's a Game?

Games begin with a setup, followed by conditions, or what we will call clues, which will apply to all of the questions with the game. The setup and clues are the rules of the game; they cannot be violated. Sometimes a question will provide an additional clue, which will only apply to that particular question, but that additional clue doesn't break the original rules. But let's not worry about questions yet. Let's get to know a game:

> A radio station will schedule five programs—A, B, C, D, and E—to be aired Monday through Friday, one program each evening, in an order that conforms to the following restrictions:
>
> Program D must be aired before Program A.
>
> Programs C and D must be aired on consecutive evenings.
>
> Program E may not be the second program to be aired.

That first paragraph is what we call the *setup*, and the restrictions are what we call the *clues*.

The Big Technique: Draw a Diagram

The only way to deal with a game is to diagram it. Get ready to use a ton of scratch paper on games—you *must* diagram everything!

Most of the games you will see on the GRE are what we call "assignment" games, meaning you're asked to assign something to something else. In the radio station example, you have to assign a program to a day of the week. So, you need to make a grid, sort of like a calendar, to represent that situation:

$$\begin{array}{|c|c|c|c|c|} \hline M & T & W & R & F \\ \hline & & & & \\ \hline \end{array}$$

Generally, you put the things that don't change at the top of the grid (days of the week don't change, but programs do). Often, things that don't change have a natural order, such as days of the week, times of day, etc. You also want to jot down the letters representing the elements, the things being assigned, or in this case, the programs: A, B, C, D, E.

You also have to diagram, or symbolize, the clues. The ability to translate the language of the clues into clear visual symbols is the key to games. You want to be able to work through the game questions using your symbols—not the words! Symbolize the clues in a way that's consistent with your diagram. Let's look at them one by one.

> Program D must be aired before
> Program A.

Because our diagram goes from left to right, "before" is the same as "to the left of" and "after" is the same as "to the right of." So, this clue can be symbolized like this:

$$D \ldots A$$

Since Program D must be aired before Program A, we put it on the left. The ellipsis (. . .) shows that D must be sometime before A, but that other programs could be aired in between those two. Next clue:

> Programs C and D must be aired on
> consecutive evenings.

We don't know which one comes first, but we do know that no program comes between C and D. So we symbolize it like this:

We put a *block* around Programs C and D to show that no other programs can be aired between those two. We also symbolize the block *both ways,* since the clue does not indicate that C must be aired before D or vice versa (don't rely on your head to remember this stuff—write everything down). Next clue:

> Program E may not be the second pro-
> gram to be aired.

Since Program E can never be the second program aired, we put that information in our model diagram to show that E can never be aired on Tuesday.

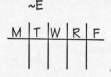

The wavy negative sign (~) means "not."

Diagramming: Wait, There's More!

We've diagrammed the setup and the clues. But we're not done. We have to double-check everything and see if there's anything else we can do to the diagram. The more you can restrict space on the diagram, the easier the game becomes. For example, because D comes sometime before A, could A ever be programmed on Monday? No, because where would you put D? So add this to your diagram:

That's called making a *deduction*. By the same token, could D ever be programmed on Friday? No, because where would you put A? So add this to your diagram:

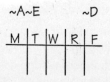

Notice that we can't make the same type of deductions with the DC/CD block, because we don't know which one comes first.

A Few Symbolizing and Deducing Guidelines

Make a separate symbol for each element: WWWW (not 4W).

When two elements are always next to each other, put a *block* around them. Blocks make games much easier. If you have elements in a block, concentrate on assigning that block instead of the individual elements. Elements in blocks are very restricted, so for deductions, think: Are there any places in the diagram where the elements in the block could never go?

When two elements can never be next to each other, use an antiblock symbol. For example, if the clue says "The apple and the pear cannot be next to each other," symbolize it like this:

$$\boxed{\cancel{AP}}$$

In some cases it's just not possible to symbolize a clue. Be sure to write some shorthand summary of the clue so that you don't forget to check that clue as you do each question.

What are your most definite clues? What are your most restricted elements? Does any element always go in one place? If so, put that element in your diagram. Are there certain places in the diagram where some elements could never go? If so, note that in those places in the diagram.

Do certain elements always have to be before other elements? If so, which places in the diagram would be closed to these elements? Make notes in your diagram.

A Special Symbol

Sometimes a clue will say something like "If B is selected, then D is selected." To symbolize that, use an arrow, like this:

$$B \longrightarrow D$$

This is called a conditional clue, or an "if . . . . then" clue. It means that whatever is on the left side of the arrow depends, or is conditional, on what's on the right side of the arrow. But whatever is on the right side of the arrow can be assigned independently.

The Contrapositive

The deduction you make from a conditional clue is called the contrapositive. You can also call it "flip and negate." For example:

> If Doug is on the team, Bill must also
> be on the team.

First symbolize: $D \longrightarrow B$

Then draw the contrapositive deduction by reversing the order of the letters and negating both letters (flip and negate):

$$\sim\!B \longrightarrow \sim\!D$$

In other words, if B is not on the team, then D cannot be on the team. This is the *only* thing that *must* follow from the clue! You may be tempted to say that if B is on the team, then D is on the team, but that's not necessarily true. B could be on the team without D. Remember, the restriction is on D, not on B. D cannot be on the team without B.

It works the same way even when the original clue includes a negative component—just like in math, negating a negative gives you a positive. For example:

> If chocolate is used, vanilla cannot be used.

You would symbolize: $C \longrightarrow \sim\!V$

And the contrapositive deduction would be: $V \longrightarrow \sim\!C$

In other words, if V *is* used, then C *cannot* be used. *Always draw the contrapositive deduction when you see "if ... then" clues.*

Don't Think—Draw!

Don't look for mental shortcuts; just get busy. Keep trying things on your scratch paper. Try one arrangement, eliminate answer choices, then try another arrangement. You'll get the right answer faster by *trying something* than by sitting and staring at the question.

Okay, let's try another one:

> Seven passengers—Jackie, Kendra, Ling, Marcus, Ned, Olivia, and Pilar—are riding on an elevator that makes four stops. Two passengers get off at every stop except the last, when the final passenger gets off. The following conditions apply:
>
> Neither Jackie nor Ned gets off with Kendra.
>
> Ling cannot get off with Marcus.
>
> Olivia must get off with either Marcus or Pilar.

Okay. The elevator makes four stops, and we're assigning passengers to stops. Keep in mind that unlike the first game we did, where there was one-to-one correspondence (five programs to five days), in this case we have seven passengers and four stops, which means that more than one person can, and will, get off at a stop. In fact, there's a clue hiding in the setup (which often happens): "Two passengers get off at every stop except the last, when the final passenger gets off." So let's set up the diagram like this:

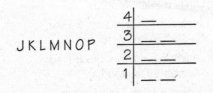

JKLMNOP

We made it vertical because it involves an elevator, but it's still a good old grid. Time for the clues:

> Neither Jackie nor Ned gets off with Kendra.

In other words, J can't get off with K, and N can't get off with K. Let's use antiblocks:

JK̶   N̶K̶

> Ling cannot get off with Marcus

Another antiblock:

L̶M̶

> Olivia must get off with either Marcus or Pilar.

In other words, O must get off with M *or* O must get off with P:

OM / MO   or   OP / PO

Now let's try a question:

> Which of the following is an acceptable list of passengers getting off the elevator, from the first stop to the last stop?
>
> ○ Jackie & Ned; Kendra & Pilar; Ling & Marcus; Olivia
>
> ○ Jackie & Ned; Kendra & Ling; Olivia & Pilar; Marcus
>
> ○ Jackie & Kendra; Ling & Pilar; Ned & Olivia; Marcus
>
> ○ Jackie & Ling; Kendra & Ned; Marcus & Olivia; Pilar
>
> ○ Jackie & Pilar; Ling & Ned Kendra & Olivia; Marcus

This is a great POE question. Take each symbol and apply it systematically to the answer choices. First we have the JK antiblock. Do any answer choices have J and K getting off together? If so, you can eliminate them. That gets rid of (C). Next, there's the NK antiblock. Do any answer choices have N and K getting off together? If so, you can eliminate them. That gets rid of (D). Next, the LM antiblock. Do any answer choices have L and M getting off together? If so, you can eliminate them. That gets rid of (A). Next, the OM or OP block. Do any answer choices have O getting off with *neither* M nor P? If so, you can eliminate them. That gets rid of (E). We're left with (B), which must be the answer. Aren't you glad you symbolized all those clues? Next question:

> If Ling gets off with Pilar, which of the following must be true?
>
> ○ Kendra gets off with Marcus.
>
> ○ Kendra gets off with Ned.
>
> ○ Jackie gets off with Marcus.
>
> ○ Kendra gets off last.
>
> ○ Jackie gets off last.

Okay, let's put this on the diagram. Since it doesn't seem to matter which stop L and P get off at (otherwise the question would mention it), let's just put them in at the first stop:

Now look at your symbols to see which ones involve the elements we've already assigned, L and P. Well, there's the OM or OP block. Now that we know P is with L, we can't have the OP block, which means we must have the OM block. Let's put it in at the second stop:

Now look at what we have left. We don't have to worry about the LM antiblock because they're already at separate stops. But we still have the JK antiblock and the NK antiblocks. If neither J nor N can get off with K, and there are only two stops left, that forces K to get off alone at the fourth stop, and puts J and N in at the third stop:

```
4| K
3| J N
2| O M
1| L P
```

Okay, now look at the answers to see which one is true; it's (D), Kendra gets off last. One more question:

> If Ling gets off last, which of the follow-
> ing passengers must get off with
> Jackie?
>
> ○ Kendra
> ○ Marcus
> ○ Ned
> ○ Olivia
> ○ Pilar

First, let's put L in the last stop:

Now, the question asks who gets off with Jackie. We can definitely eliminate (A), because there's a JK antiblock. Now we have to keep our pencils moving and try stuff. Let's start with the blocks because they're the most restrictive. We know that there has to be either an OM block or an OP block. Let's see what happens with the OM block first—put it in at the first stop (though it doesn't matter which stop you put it at). Since neither J nor N can be with K, and there are only two stops left, we have to put J and N together at one of the remaining stops, and that leaves K and P for the other remaining stop:

So, in this scenario, N got off with J. It's safe to pick (C), but maybe you're skeptical because we randomly started with the OM block and not the OP block. Just because you're new at this, let's see what happens with the OP block—put it in at the first stop (though it doesn't matter which stop you put it at), and don't forget to put L in at the last stop again (as the question dictates). Again, since neither J nor N can be with K, and there are only two stops left, we have to put J and N together at one of the remaining stops, and that leaves K and M for the other remaining stop:

But on test day, once you get an answer, pick it and move on—don't try a million possibilities, or you'll never finish. Be confident in the choice you make.

A Different Diagram—the Map Game

In an assignment game, which the majority of GRE games are, you assign elements to places. In a map game, which you might see on your test, there are no places to put the elements. Rather, the setup of the game describes *something moving* among the elements, or *connections* between the elements. Take the time to symbolize the clues carefully, then combine the clues into one diagram that incorporates all the information. Double-checking before you go to the questions is especially crucial. Let's look at one:

> In a message relay system there are exactly seven terminals—F, G, H, J, K, L, and M. A terminal can transmit any messages initiated by that terminal as well as any messages received from others, but only according to specific rules:
>
> Messages can be transmitted in either direction between G and H, in either direction between J and M, and in either direction between K and L.
>
> Messages can be transmitted from F to K, from H to J, from K to G, from M to F, and from M to H.

See how you can't really make a grid here, because there's no place to put the elements? But you can indicate the connections between the elements. You'll have to symbolize the clues first, and then put them all together to make your map diagram. Here's the first clue again:

> Messages can be transmitted in either direction between G and H, in either direction between J and M, and in either direction between K and L.

Diagram it like this:

$$G \longleftrightarrow H$$

$$J \longleftrightarrow M$$

$$K \longleftrightarrow L$$

Notice the arrows are going in both directions, like the clue says. Here's the next clue:

> Messages can be transmitted from F to K, from H to J, from K to G, from M to F, and from M to H.

Diagram it like this:

$$F \longrightarrow K$$

$$H \longrightarrow J$$

$$K \longrightarrow G$$

$$M \longrightarrow F$$

$$M \longrightarrow H$$

Note that these are not the same as those "if . . . then" arrows. In map games, they are *directional* arrows. Note also that these arrows are going in one direction, like the clue says. Now you have to string these little connections into one big connection. Just start with one and link them together. Write down the G to H connection, then add whatever connects to the G and whatever connects to the H, till you've got them all:

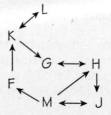

Don't worry if you're diagram doesn't look exactly like this; as long as the connections are the same. Okay, let's look at a question:

Which of the seven terminals can trans-
mit messages directly to the greatest
number of terminals?

○ F

○ H

○ J

○ K

○ M

This question is really asking, "Which terminal is connected to the
most terminals?" Just look at your diagram and count, remembering
that some of those arrows only go in one direction, so you only need
to count the connections that are coming *from* a terminal. Let's go
through the answers:

(A) F transmits to K; that's 1.

(B) H transmits to G and J; that's 2.

(C) J transmits to M; that's 1.

(D) K transmits to G and L; that's 2.

(E) M transmits to F, H, and J; that's 3, and that's the answer.

Here's another question:

If a message initiated by G is to reach
K, and is to be transmitted to no more
terminals than necessary, it must be
transmitted to a total of how many terminals other than G and K?

○ 1

○ 2

○ 3

○ 4

○ 5

We have to get from G to K; just trace that path on your diagram: G $\longrightarrow$ H $\longrightarrow$ J $\longrightarrow$ M $\longrightarrow$ F $\longrightarrow$ K. So, other than G and K, the message was transmitted to four terminals. That's (D). One more question:

> A message from H that eventually reaches L must have been transmitted to all of the following terminals EXCEPT
>
> ○ F
> ○ G
> ○ J
> ○ K
> ○ M

We have to get from H to L; just trace that path on your diagram: H $\longrightarrow$ J $\longrightarrow$ M $\longrightarrow$ F $\longrightarrow$ K $\longrightarrow$ L. Since this is an EXCEPT question, we're looking for the terminal that the message *wasn't* transmitted to, so we can eliminate any choices containing terminals it *was* transmitted to. That eliminates (A), (C), (D), and (E). The answer is (B).

PART

DRILLS

These drills are divided into sets that correspond with the chapters in the book. Practice the math drills *after* you've read *all* of the math chapters, because some questions corresponding with one chapter might require you to use techniques from another chapter.

Remember, don't do any work in this book. Use scratch paper, just like on test day. Here we go!

VERBAL

Analogies

1. CHOREOGRAPHER : DANCE ::
   - Ⓐ connoisseur : art
   - Ⓑ composer : music
   - Ⓒ acrobat : height
   - Ⓓ athlete : contest
   - Ⓔ virtuoso : skill

2. SCOWL : DISPLEASURE ::
   - Ⓐ sing : praise
   - Ⓑ kiss : affection
   - Ⓒ confess : crime
   - Ⓓ irritate : anger
   - Ⓔ hurl : disgust

3. GOGGLES : EYES ::
   - Ⓐ tie : neck
   - Ⓑ gloves : hands
   - Ⓒ elbow : arm
   - Ⓓ braid : hair
   - Ⓔ splint : leg

4. DRAWL : SPEAK ::
   - Ⓐ spurt : expel
   - Ⓑ foster : develop
   - Ⓒ scintillate : flash
   - Ⓓ pare : trim
   - Ⓔ saunter : walk

5. ARBORETUM : TREE ::
   (A) dam : water
   (B) planetarium : star
   (C) apiary : bee
   (D) museum : painting
   (E) forum : speech

6. GALL : IRRITATION :.
   (A) accommodate : deception
   (B) beleaguer : felicity
   (C) awe : apathy
   (D) discomfit : confusion
   (E) inculcate : fear

7. SUBTERFUGE : DECEIVE ::
   (A) decanter : pour
   (B) interview : hire
   (C) account : save
   (D) outpost : protect
   (E) film : view

8. RATIFY : APPROVAL ::
   (A) mutate : change
   (B) pacify : conquest
   (C) duel : combat
   (D) appeal : authority
   (E) tribulate : opinion

9. SOPORIFIC : SLEEP ::
   (A) conductor : electricity
   (B) syncopation : beat
   (C) provocation : debate
   (D) coagulant : blood
   (E) astringent : pucker

10. METTLESOME : COURAGE :.
  Ⓐ audacious : tenacity
  Ⓑ mediocre : originality
  Ⓒ ludicrous : inanity
  Ⓓ dubious : suspiciousness
  Ⓔ altruistic : donation

Sentence Completions

1. It is the concern of many ecologists that the "greenhouse effect" is changing many of the Earth's _____ weather patterns into _____ systems, unable to be accurately forecast by those who study them.
  Ⓐ predictable . . erratic
  Ⓑ steady . . growing
  Ⓒ uncertain . . uncanny
  Ⓓ chaotic . . unforeseeable
  Ⓔ weighty . . unbounded

2. Children, after more than a generation of television, have become "hasty viewers"; as a result, if the camera lags, the attention of these young viewers _____.
  Ⓐ expands
  Ⓑ starts
  Ⓒ alternates
  Ⓓ wanes
  Ⓔ clarifies

3. Many of the troubles and deficiencies in otherwise thriving foreign enterprises are _____ ignored or diminished by the author of the article in order to _____ the ways in which other businesses might attempt to imitate them.
  Ⓐ unintentionally . . overstate
  Ⓑ deliberately . . stress
  Ⓒ intermittently . . equalize
  Ⓓ willfully . . confound
  Ⓔ brilliantly . . illustrate

4. Frequently a copyright holder's property, published articles for example, is reproduced repeatedly in the absence of _____ for its reproduction, an action _____ by long-standing practice.

  (A) validation . . provoked
  (B) recognition . . forecast
  (C) payment . . licensed
  (D) accommodation . . instigated
  (E) allowance . . aggravated

5. After screenwriter Neil Jordan's most recent work opened in selected urban areas, many theatergoers were _____, but after pundits expressed their _____, appreciation of the film increased and distribution surged.

  (A) skeptical . . approbation
  (B) apathetic . . diffidence
  (C) ebullient . . trepidation
  (D) dubious . . disdain
  (E) unimpressed . . antipathy

6. The pieces exhibited at many university galleries are chosen to reflect the diverse tastes of the academic communities they serve; the curators avoid _____ in favor of _____.

  (A) continuity . . rigidity
  (B) variation . . craftsmanship
  (C) uniformity . . eclecticism
  (D) modernism . . classics
  (E) homogeneity . . segmentation

7. The American public venerates medical researchers because the researchers make frequent discoveries of tremendous humanitarian consequence; however, the daily routines of scientists are largely made up of result verification and statistical analysis, making their occupation seem _____.

Ⓐ fascinating
Ⓑ quotidian
Ⓒ recalcitrant
Ⓓ experimental
Ⓔ amorphous

8. The _____ of early metaphysicians' efforts to decipher the workings of the universe led some later thinkers to question the _____ of man's intellectual capabilities.

Ⓐ strain . . roots
Ⓑ intent . . superiority
Ⓒ intricacy . . realization
Ⓓ prevarications . . deceptiveness
Ⓔ failings . . adeptness

9. Being gracious should not be mistaken for a _____ characteristic of men's personalities; it is instead a fundamental virtue, one whose very state of being is increasingly _____ by the fashionable directive to "say what you feel."

Ⓐ trivial . . imperiled
Ⓑ pervading . . undermined
Ⓒ frivolous . . averted
Ⓓ superior . . renounced
Ⓔ immaterial . . influenced

10. While some individuals think that the purpose of sarcastic remarks is to disturb, by turning all communication into _____, other people see sarcastic remarks as a desire for supremacy in miniature over an environment that appears too _____.

- (A) chaos . . perplexed
- (B) equivalence . . confused
- (C) discord . . amiable
- (D) pandemonium . . disorderly
- (E) similarity . . upset

Antonyms

1. SLUR:
   - (A) honor agreements
   - (B) settle disputes
   - (C) pronounce clearly
   - (D) criticize directly
   - (E) exclude purposefully

2. MORATORIUM:
   - (A) lack of emotion
   - (B) discouragement
   - (C) savings
   - (D) brilliance
   - (E) period of activity

3. DIFFUSE:
   - (A) compare
   - (B) chill
   - (C) concentrate
   - (D) blemish
   - (E) oscillate

4. THWART:
   - (A) aid
   - (B) beseech
   - (C) dislocate
   - (D) assign
   - (E) allege

5. AGITATE:
   - Ⓐ relieve
   - Ⓑ satisfy
   - Ⓒ reject
   - Ⓓ vcondense
   - Ⓔ confirm

6. AUTHENTICATE:
   - Ⓐ sentence
   - Ⓑ disseminate
   - Ⓒ scrutinize
   - Ⓓ theorize
   - Ⓔ discredit

7. ACCLIMATION:
   - Ⓐ alienation
   - Ⓑ adoration
   - Ⓒ facilitation
   - Ⓓ invigoration
   - Ⓔ exaltation

8. TENUOUSLY:
   - Ⓐ having a strong basis
   - Ⓑ following a formal procedure
   - Ⓒ having overall consensus
   - Ⓓ with evil intent
   - Ⓔ under loose supervision

9. FLORID:
   - Ⓐ pallid
   - Ⓑ vapid
   - Ⓒ lucid
   - Ⓓ vrancid
   - Ⓔ candid

10. MISCIBLE:
    - Ⓐ likely to agree
    - Ⓑ hard to please
    - Ⓒ generous
    - Ⓓ desirable
    - Ⓔ not capable of being mixed

Reading Comprehension

Questions 1–7

Although the study of women's history has only been developed as an academic discipline in the last twenty years, it is not the case that the current wave of feminist activity is the first in which interest in
5 women's past was manifest. From its very beginnings, the nineteenth-century English women's movement sought to expand existing knowledge of the activities and achievements of women in the past. At the same time, like its American counterpart, the English
10 women's movement had a powerful sense of its own historic importance and of its relationship to wider social and political change.

Nowhere is this sense of the historical importance— and of the historical connections between the women's
15 movement and other social and political develop- ments—more evident than in Ray Strachey's classic account of the movement, *The Cause*. "The true history of the Women's Movement," Strachey argues, "is the whole history of the nineteenth century." The women's
20 movement was part of the broad sweep of liberal and progressive reform that was transforming society. Strachey emphasized this connection between the women's movement and the broader sweep of history by highlighting the influence of the Enlightenment and
25 the Industrial Revolution on it. The protest made by the women's movement at the confinement and injustices faced by women was, in Strachey's view, part of the liberal attack on traditional prejudices and injustice. This critique of women's confinement was supple-
30 mented by the demand for recognition of women's role

in the public, particularly the philanthropic, realm.
Indeed, it was the criticism of the limitations faced by
women on the one hand, and their establishment of a
new public role on the other hand, that provided the
35 core of the movement, determining also its form: its
organization around campaigns for legal, political, and
social reform.

Strachey's analysis was a very illuminating one,
nowhere more so than in her insistence that, despite
40 their differences and even antipathy to each other,
both the radical Mary Wollstonecraft and evangelical
Hannah More need to be seen as forerunners of mid-
Victorian feminism. At the same time, she omitted
some issues that now seem crucial to any discussion
45 of the context of Victorian feminism. Where Strachey
pictured a relatively fixed image of domestic women
throughout the first half of the nineteenth century,
recent historical and literary works suggest that this
image was both complex and unstable. The establish-
50 ment of a separate domestic sphere for women was
but one aspect of the enormous change in sexual and
familial relationships that were occurring from the late
eighteenth through the mid-nineteenth century. These
changes were accompanied by both anxiety and
55 uncertainty and by the constant articulation of
women's duty in a new social world.

1. The primary purpose of the passage is to

Ⓐ present an overview of the economic
changes that led to the English
women's movement

Ⓑ evaluate a view of the English women's
movement as presented in a literary work

Ⓒ describe the social and political context
of the women's movement in England

Ⓓ voffer a novel analysis of England's
reaction to the women's movement

Ⓔ profile several of the women who were
instrumental in the success of the
English women's movement

2. Which of the following is the best description of Ray Strachey's work, *The Cause*?

  Ⓐ historical analysis of a social movement

  Ⓑ a critique of an important feminist text

  Ⓒ a feminist revision of accepted history

  Ⓓ a novel written as social commentary

  Ⓔ a treatise on women's issues in the 1900s

3. The passage contains information to answer all of the following questions EXCEPT

  Ⓐ In what respect were the goals of the women's movement in England similar to those of the women's movement in America?

  Ⓑ How were the emphases of the women's movement compatible with the liberal ideals of nineteenth-century England?

  Ⓒ In what way was the political orientation of Mary Wollstonecraft different from that of Ray Strachey?

  Ⓓ By what means did participants in the women's movement in England seek to achieve their goals?

  Ⓔ What historical movements were taking place at the same time as the women's movement in England?

4. The author includes Strachey's claim that "the true history of the Women's Movement . . . is the whole history of the nineteenth century" (lines 17–19) in order to emphasize

    Ⓐ Strachey's belief that the advancement of women's rights was the most significant development of its century

    Ⓑ the importance Strachey attributes to the women's movement in bringing about the Enlightenment

    Ⓒ Strachey's awareness of the interconnection of the women's movement and other societal changes in the 1800s

    Ⓓ Strachey's contention that the women's movement, unlike other social and political developments of the time, actually transformed society

    Ⓔ Strachey's argument that the nineteenth century must play a role in any criticism of the limitations of women

5. While the author acknowledges Strachey's importance in the study of women's history, she faults Strachey for

    Ⓐ focusing her study on the legal and political reform enacted by the women's movement

    Ⓑ oversimplifying her conception of the social condition of women prior to the reforms of the women's movement

    Ⓒ failing to eliminate the anachronistic idea of "women's duty" from her articulation of nineteenth-century feminism

    Ⓓ omitting Mary Wollstonecraft and Hannah More from her discussion of important influences in feminism

    Ⓔ recommending a static and domestic social role for women following the women's movement

6. The author's attitude toward Strachey's analysis is one of

Ⓐ qualified admiration

Ⓑ optimistic enthusiasm

Ⓒ extreme criticism

Ⓓ studied impartiality

Ⓔ intellectual curiosity

7. Which of the following, if true, would most weaken the author's assertion about the similarity between the English and American women's movements?

Ⓐ The English and American women's movements took place in very different sociohistorical climates.

Ⓑ The English women's movement began almost a century before the American women's movement.

Ⓒ The English women's movement excluded men, while the American women's movement did not.

Ⓓ Few members of the English women's movement were aware of the impact it would have on society.

Ⓔ Many participants in the English women's movement continued to perform traditional domestic roles.

Questions 8–10

Following the discovery in 1895 that malaria is carried by Anopheles mosquitoes, governments around the world set out to eradicate those insect vectors. In Europe, the relation between the malarial agent, pro-
5 tozoan blood parasites of the genus Plasmodium, and the vector mosquito, *Anopheles maculipennis*, seemed at first inconsistent. In some localities the mosquito was abundant but malaria rare or absent, while in others the reverse was true. In 1934 the prob-
10 lem was solved. Entomologists discovered that A.

maculipennis is not a single species but a group of at least seven.

In outward appearance the adult mosquitoes seem almost identical, but in fact they are marked by a host
15 of distinctive biological traits, some of which prevent them from hybridizing. Some of the species distinguished by these traits were found to feed on human blood and thus to carry the malarial parasites. Once identified, the dangerous members of the *A. mac-*
20 *ulipennis* complex could be targeted and eradicated.

8. Which of the following best expresses the author's main point in the passage above?

Ⓐ With the increasing density of the human population, it will become increasingly necessary to reduce populations of other species.

Ⓑ Without an understanding of the seven groups of *A. maculipennis* mosquitoes, eradication of malaria will be unlikely.

Ⓒ Despite the eradication of large numbers of Plasmodium-carrying mosquitoes, malaria is still a significant problem in certain localities.

Ⓓ After establishing the relationship between Plasmodium and the vector mosquito, scientists discovered that *Anopheles* mosquitoes carried malaria.

Ⓔ To eradicate an insect disease vector, it was necessary to have a scientific understanding of that vector.

9. Which of the following best describes the reason that scientists were initially perplexed at the discovery that malaria was spread by *Anopheles* mosquitoes?

Ⓐ Scientists had evidence that malaria was carried by the protozoan blood parasite Plasmodium.

Ⓑ Scientists felt that because so many species of *Anopheles* existed, they could not be carriers.

Ⓒ Scientists were unable to find a direct correlation between *Anopheles* density and frequency of malaria occurrence.

Ⓓ Scientists knew that many species of *Anopheles* mosquito did not feed on human blood.

Ⓔ Scientists believed that the *Anopheles* mosquito could not be host to the parasite Plasmodium.

10. It can be inferred from the passage that a mosquito becomes a carrier of malaria when

Ⓐ it ingests the blood of a human being infected with malaria

Ⓑ it lives in regions where malaria is widespread

Ⓒ it consumes blood from a protozoan malarial agent

Ⓓ it has extended contact with other insect vectors

Ⓔ it is spawned in Plasmodium-infested localities

MATH

Numbers

Column A	Column B
1. $4[(3 + 3) + 4]$	45

- Ⓐ the quantity in Column A is always greater
- Ⓑ the quantity in Column B is always greater
- Ⓒ the quantities are always equal
- Ⓓ different numbers would result in different answers

Column A	Column B
2. $\dfrac{8}{9}$	$\dfrac{7}{8}$

- Ⓐ the quantity in Column A is always greater
- Ⓑ the quantity in Column B is always greater
- Ⓒ the quantities are always equal
- Ⓓ different numbers would result in different answers

3. What is the remainder when 117 is divided by 3?

- Ⓐ 3
- Ⓑ 2
- Ⓒ 1
- Ⓓ $\dfrac{1}{2}$
- Ⓔ 0

Column A	Column B

4. The units digit in the number 1,743 | The hundreds digit in the number 5,243

  Ⓐ the quantity in Column A is always greater

  Ⓑ the quantity in Column B is always greater

  Ⓒ the quantities are always equal

  Ⓓ different numbers would result in different answers

Column A	Column B

$$1.3 + .6 + .9 + x = 5$$

5. x 2.3

  Ⓐ the quantity in Column A is always greater

  Ⓑ the quantity in Column B is always greater

  Ⓒ the quantities are always equal

  Ⓓ different numbers would result in different answers

Column A	Column B

6. $4(2^6)$ $6(4^2)$

  Ⓐ the quantity in Column A is always greater

  Ⓑ the quantity in Column B is always greater

  Ⓒ the quantities are always equal

  Ⓓ different numbers would result in different answers

Column A	Column B

7. $\sqrt{\dfrac{7}{3}}$ $\dfrac{1}{3}\sqrt{7}$

Ⓐ the quantity in Column A is always greater

Ⓑ the quantity in Column B is always greater

Ⓒ the quantities are always equal

Ⓓ different numbers would result in different answers

Column A	Column B

Mr. Jones purchased a new bedroom set by using an extended payment plan. The regular price of the set was $900, but on the payment plan he paid $300 up front and 9 monthly payments of $69 each.

8. $23   The amount Mr. Jones paid in addition to the regular price of the bedroom set

Ⓐ the quantity in Column A is always greater

Ⓑ the quantity in Column B is always greater

Ⓒ the quantities are always equal

Ⓓ different numbers would result in different answers

9. Which of the following is NOT an integer if
$K = 21 \times 54 \times 22$?

Ⓐ $\dfrac{K}{21}$

Ⓑ $\dfrac{K}{27}$

Ⓒ $\dfrac{K}{48}$

Ⓓ $\dfrac{K}{33}$

Ⓔ $\dfrac{K}{63}$

Column A	Column B
10. $3^{17} + 3^{18}$	$(4)3^{17}$

Ⓐ the quantity in Column A is always greater

Ⓑ the quantity in Column B is always greater

Ⓒ the quantities are always equal

Ⓓ different numbers would result in different answers

Figures

Column A   Column B

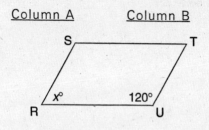

RSTU is a parallelogram

1.   *x*   45

    Ⓐ the quantity in Column A is always greater

    Ⓑ the quantity in Column B is always greater

    Ⓒ the quantities are always equal

    Ⓓ different numbers would result in different answers

2. A pie is baked in a circular plate with a radius of 6 inches. If the pie is then cut into eight equal pieces, what would be the area, in square inches, of each slice of the pie?

    Ⓐ $\frac{1}{8}\pi$

    Ⓑ $\frac{2}{9}\pi$

    Ⓒ $\frac{9}{2}\pi$

    Ⓓ 6π

    Ⓔ 36π

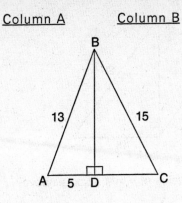

Column A   Column B

3. The perimeter of   42
   triangle BCD

   Ⓐ the quantity in Column A is always
      greater
   Ⓑ the quantity in Column B is always
      greater
   Ⓒ the quantities are always equal
   Ⓓ different numbers would result in dif-
      ferent answers

4. In the figure above, what does b equal if
   $a = 3b$?

   Ⓐ 40
   Ⓑ 30
   Ⓒ 25
   Ⓓ 20
   Ⓔ 10

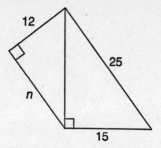

5. What is the value of *n* in the figure above?
    (A) 9
    (B) 15
    (C) 16
    (D) $12\sqrt{3}$
    (E) 20

6. What is the perimeter, in centimeters, of a rectangular newspaper ad 14 centimeters wide that has the same area as a rectangular newspaper ad 52 centimeters long and 28 centimeters wide?
    (A)　80
    (B) 118
    (C) 160
    (D) 208
    (E) 236

Column A   Column B

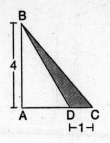

Triangle ABC is isosceles.

7. The area of the shaded $\dfrac{1}{3}$
    region in ABC divided
    by the area of the
    unshaded region in
    ABC

    Ⓐ the quantity in Column A is always
       greater
    Ⓑ the quantity in Column B is always
       greater
    Ⓒ the quantities are always equal
    Ⓓ different numbers would result in dif-
       ferent answers

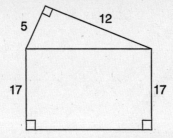

Note: Figure is not drawn to scale.

8. What is the perimeter of the figure above?

Ⓐ 51
Ⓑ 64
Ⓒ 68
Ⓓ 77
Ⓔ 91

<u>Column A</u>   <u>Column B</u>

The circumference of a circle with a radius

of $\frac{1}{2}$ meter is C meters.

9. C 4

Ⓐ the quantity in Column A is always greater
Ⓑ the quantity in Column B is always greater
Ⓓ the quantities are always equal
Ⓔ different numbers would result in different answers

Column A   Column B

10. The circumference The perimeter of a
of a circular region square with side r
with radius r

Ⓐ the quantity in Column A is always
greater

Ⓑ the quantity in Column B is always
greater

Ⓒ the quantities are always equal

Ⓓ different numbers would result in different answers

Equations I

Column A   Column B

1. 30 percent of $150 60 percent of $75

Ⓐ the quantity in Column A is always
greater

Ⓑ the quantity in Column B is always
greater

Ⓒ the quantities are always equal

Ⓓ different numbers would result in different answers

Column A   Column B

The average (arithmetic mean) of two positive integers is equal to 17. Each of the integers is greater than 12.

2. Twice the larger of   44
the two integers

Ⓐ the quantity in Column A is always
greater

Ⓑ the quantity in Column B is always
greater

Ⓒ the quantities are always equal

Ⓓ different numbers would result in different answers

3. If the cost of a one-hour telephone call is $7.20, what would be the cost of a ten-minute telephone call at the same rate?

   Ⓐ $7.10
   Ⓑ $3.60
   Ⓒ $1.80
   Ⓓ $1.20
   Ⓔ $ .72

Column A	Column B

4. The average (arithmetic mean) of 7, 3, 4, and 2   The average (arithmetic mean) of $2a + 5$, $4a$, and $7 - 6a$

   Ⓐ the quantity in Column A is always greater
   Ⓑ the quantity in Column B is always greater
   Ⓒ the quantities are always equal
   Ⓓ different numbers would result in different answers

Column A	Column B

A discount of 30 percent followed by a discount of 25 percent would equal a single discount of p percent.

5. p 47.5

   Ⓐ the quantity in Column A is always greater
   Ⓑ the quantity in Column B is always greater
   Ⓒ the quantities are always equal
   Ⓓ different numbers would result in different answers

6. If $m + n = p$, then $m^2 + 2mn + n^2 =$

    Ⓐ $4p$

    Ⓑ $np - m$

    Ⓒ p^2

    Ⓓ $p^2 + 4(m + p)$

    Ⓔ $p^2 + np + m^2$

7. For all real numbers x and y, if
$x * y = x(x - y)$, then $x * (x * y) =$

    Ⓐ $x^2 - xy$

    Ⓑ $x^2 - 2xy$

    Ⓒ $x^3 - x^2 - xy$

    Ⓓ $x^3 - (xy)^2$

    Ⓔ $x^2 - x^3 + x^2y$

Questions 8–10 refer to the following charts.

PRIVATE DONATIONS TO CHARITABLE CAUSES IN COUNTRY X, Jan. 1971-Dec.1989

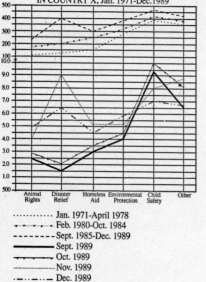

DISTRIBUTION OF CHARITABLE ORGANIZATION COUNTRY X BY CAUSE, Sept. 1989

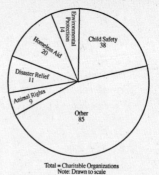

Total = Charitable Organizations
Note: Drawn to scale

·············· Jan. 1971-April 1978
–•–•–•– Feb. 1980-Oct. 1984
– – – – – Sept. 1985-Dec. 1989
———— Sept. 1989
–•——•– Oct. 1989
················ Nov. 1989
–••–••– Dec. 1989

8. Which of the following categories of charitable causes received the third greatest amount in private donations from January 1971 to April 1978?

Ⓐ Disaster relief

Ⓑ Homeless aid

Ⓒ Environmental protection

Ⓓ Child safety

Ⓔ "Other" causes

9. If funds contributed to child safety organizations in September 1989 were distributed evenly to those organizations, approximately how much did each charity receive?

Ⓐ $12,000,000

Ⓑ $9,400,000

Ⓒ $2,500,000

Ⓓ $250,000

Ⓔ $38,000

10. From September 1985 to December 1989, what was the approximate ratio of private donations in millions to homeless aid to private donations in millions to animal rights?

Ⓐ 20:9

Ⓑ 3:2

Ⓒ 4:3

Ⓓ 9:7

Ⓔ 6:5

Equations II

1. Alex gave Jonathan a dollars. She gave Gina two dollars more than she gave Jonathan and she gave Louanne three dollars less than she gave Gina. In terms of a, how many dollars did Alex give Gina, Jonathan, and Louanne altogether?

Ⓐ $\frac{a}{3}$

Ⓑ $a - 1$

Ⓒ $3a$

Ⓓ $3a - 1$

Ⓔ $3a + 1$

2. If $3x = -2$, then $(3x - 3)^2 =$

Ⓐ -9

Ⓑ -6

Ⓒ -1

Ⓓ 25

Ⓔ 36

3. Mike bought a used car and had it repainted. If the cost of the paint job was one-fifth of the purchase price of the car, and if the cost of the car and the paint job combined was $4,800, then what was the purchase price of the car?

    Ⓐ $800

    Ⓑ $960

    Ⓒ $3,840

    Ⓓ $4,000

    Ⓔ $4,250

4. If $x + y = z$ and $x = y$, then all of the following are true EXCEPT

    Ⓐ $2x + 2y = 2z$

    Ⓑ $x - y = 0$

    Ⓒ $x - z = y - z$

    Ⓓ $x = \dfrac{z}{2}$

    Ⓔ $x - y = 2z$

5. If x and y are integers and xy is an even integer, which of the following must be an odd integer?

    Ⓐ $xy + 5$

    Ⓑ $x + y$

    Ⓒ $\dfrac{x}{y}$

    Ⓓ $4x$

    Ⓔ $7xy$

6. What is the least number r for which $(3r + 2)(r - 3) = 0$?

Ⓐ –3

Ⓑ –2

Ⓒ $-\dfrac{2}{3}$

Ⓓ $\dfrac{2}{3}$

Ⓔ 3

Column A	Column B
7. $x + 1$	$1 - x$

Ⓐ the quantity in Column A is always greater

Ⓑ the quantity in Column B is always greater

Ⓒ the quantities are always equal

Ⓓ different numbers would result in different answers

8. A restaurant owner sold 2 dishes to each of his customers at $4 per dish. At the end of the day, he had taken in $180, which included $20 in tips. How many customers did he serve?

Ⓐ 18

Ⓑ 20

Ⓒ 22

Ⓓ 40

Ⓔ 44

Column A   Column B

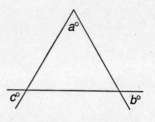

9. $b + c$ $180 - a$

Ⓐ the quantity in Column A is always greater

Ⓑ the quantity in Column B is always greater

Ⓒ the quantities are always equal

Ⓓ different numbers would result in different answers

10. In a certain election, 60 percent of the voters were women. If 30 percent of the women and 20 percent of the men voted for candidate X, what percent of all the voters in that election voted for candidate X?

Ⓐ 18%

Ⓑ 25%

Ⓒ 26%

Ⓓ 30%

Ⓔ 50%

ANALYTIC

Arguments

1. Over the past five years, Clean toothpaste has been advertised as the most effective means of preventing tooth decay. However, according to dentists' records, many patients experiencing severe tooth decay used Clean toothpaste. Clearly, Clean toothpaste is not an effective means of preventing tooth decay.

   Which of the following statements, if true, would most seriously weaken the conclusion above?

   Ⓐ Of the patients experiencing tooth decay, two-thirds indicate that they would be willing to switch brands of toothpaste.

   Ⓑ The advertisements for Clean toothpaste advocate brushing twice a day.

   Ⓒ If Clean toothpaste were not available, more patients would experience severe tooth decay.

   Ⓓ Dentists continue to recommend Clean toothpaste more than any other brand.

   Ⓔ Of those who experienced severe tooth decay, only one-eighth also experienced gum disease.

2. For five years, while remodeling the town zoo, the Rogerton Parks Commission has been transferring a large number of animals from the city of Rogerton to both the Stilton and Bailey Zoos in the city of Garroville. It follows that when Rogerton's zoo reopens next year, either Stilton or Bailey will have to be closed and their animal populations consolidated.

The author of the statements above assumes that

Ⓐ the removal of the Rogerton animals from the Stilton and Bailey Zoos will leave one or both of these Zoos considerably underpopulated.

Ⓑ Rogerton's remodeled zoo will not be large enough for the prospective animal population.

Ⓒ the Rogerton animals comprise only a small part of the total animal populations at both the Stilton and Bailey Zoos.

Ⓓ incorporation of extra animals from Rogerton has placed a tremendous burden on the resources of both the Stilton and Bailey Zoos.

Ⓔ animals will not be sent between the Stilton and Bailey Zoos in the next year.

3. A group of physicians wishing to explore the link between protein intake and high blood pressure performed a nutrition experiment on a selected group of ten vegetarians. Five of the people were given a high-protein, low-fat diet. The group given the high-protein, low-fat diet exhibited the same 5 percent increase in blood pressure as did the group given the low-protein, high-fat diet.

Which of the following conclusions can most properly be drawn if the statements above are true?

Ⓐ The physicians did not establish a link between protein intake and high blood pressure.

Ⓑ The sample chosen by the physicians was not representative of the general vegetarian population.

© Some physicians believe there is a link between protein intake and high blood pressure.

① Vegetarians are more likely to eat a high-protein, low-fat diet than a low-protein, high-fat diet.

⑤ There is a link between protein intake and high blood pressure.

4. Whenever Joe does his laundry at the Main Street Laundromat, the loads turn out cleaner than they do when he does his laundry at the Elm Street Laundromat. Laundry done at the Main Street Laundromat is cleaner because the machines at the Main Street Laundromat use more water per load than do those at the Elm Street Laundromat.

Which of the following statements, if true, helps support the conclusion above?

Ⓐ The clothes washed at the Elm Street Laundromat were, overall, less clean than those washed at the Main Street Laundromat.

Ⓑ Joe uses the same detergent at both laundromats.

© The machines at the Elm Street Laundromat use twice as much water as do those at the Main Street Laundromat.

① Joe does three times as much laundry at the Main Street Laundromat as he does at the Elm Street Laundromat.

⑤ Joe tends to do his dirtier laundry at the Elm Street Laundromat.

5. A man-made plant hormone has been added to a section of a garden in order to ward off insect infestation. The designer of the hormone has asserted that the recent dearth of insects in that section of the garden demonstrates that the man-made plant hormone wards off insect infestation.

Which of the following, if true, would cast the greatest doubt on the designer's assertion?

Ⓐ The recent dearth of insects in that section of the garden was not as complete as had been expected given the results derived in controlled experiments.

Ⓑ Because the man-made plant hormone would ultimately be neutralized by soil erosion, more man-made plant hormones would need to be added to the garden every three months.

Ⓒ A man-made plant hormone produced from different chemicals had been developed by the designer at an earlier period was ineffective in warding off insect infestation.

Ⓓ The recent dearth of insects in that section of the garden is the same as the recent dearth of insects in otherwise very similar sections of the garden without the man-made plant hormone.

Ⓔ The recent dearth of insects in that section of the garden, even though substantial, is not yet sufficient to compensate for the plant loss in that section of the garden in the last year.

6. A higher level of safety in automotive braking mechanisms depends upon control by internal computer monitoring systems. Automotive braking mechanisms, to be safe, would have to pump in intervals, and determining that the brakes would compensate for all situations is impossible. Despite technological advances, every internal computer monitoring system has on use proved to have serious weaknesses that in certain circumstances would bring about significant failure.

Which of the following can be inferred from the statements above?

Ⓐ If designers are diligent in planning the internal computer monitoring system to be used for automotive braking mechanisms, there is an exceptionally good chance that the braking mechanism will ensure a high level of safety if and when it is needed.

Ⓑ Techniques for decreasing the number of errors in building internal computer monitoring systems will not be discovered.

Ⓒ Automotive braking mechanisms will not function safely during pumping.

Ⓓ Some method of control other than internal computer monitoring systems will have to be designed.

Ⓔ The safety of automobile braking systems cannot be ensured during pumping.

7. During the past fifteen years, 20 percent of the judges with sufficient experience to be considered for federal judgeships were women, and all of those deemed to have sufficient experience during those years received federal judgeships. Despite this fact, only 8 percent of federal judgeships are currently filled by women.

Which of the following, if true, could explain the discrepancy in the percentages cited in the passage above?

Ⓐ Fifteen years ago, it required less experience to be considered for federal judgeships than it does today.

Ⓑ The majority of those holding federal judgeships have held those positions for more than fifteen years, dating back to a time when practically everyone holding that position was male.

Ⓒ The women with sufficient experience to be considered for federal judgeships have tended to specialize in different areas of law than the men considered for federal judgeships.

Ⓓ Men and women holding federal judgeships have received equal financial compensation for the previous fifteen years.

Ⓔ Although women currently hold eight percent of the federal judgeships, they hold only three percent of circuit judgeships.

8. It has been argued that medical researchers would make more impressive strides in their effort to develop cures for certain infectious diseases if they knew more about how cells replicate. This argument, however, could be challenged on the basis that a major advance in pest control has never come from any insight into the reproductive patterns of insects.

The argument above relies on an analogy that assumes that fighting infectious diseases is an endeavor similar to which of the following?

Ⓐ theories of cell replication

Ⓑ efforts at pest control

Ⓒ conclusions about how researchers make advances

Ⓓ patterns of infectious disease transmission in insects

Ⓔ research into the reproductive patterns of insects

9. Collies are the most frequently purchased dogs at dog breeding farms. Clearly, collies' superior performance in dog shows makes them popular dogs to buy as pets.

Which of the following, if true, would most seriously weaken the claim made above?

Ⓐ Collies require less food and care than do most other dogs.

Ⓑ It is because of their glossy fur that collies place well in dog shows.

Ⓒ Public interest in dog shows has been surging in the recent past.

Ⓓ Schnauzers generally place "best in show" and they are extremely popular dogs to buy as pets.

Ⓔ Dogs that place well in shows invariably are the most popular dogs to buy as pets.

10. There are more than fifty furniture stores in Middle Valley and not one of them charges less for furniture than does Green's Furniture Warehouse. It is clear that Green's Furniture Warehouse is the store that will provide the lowest price for furniture in all of Middle Valley.

Which of the following is an assumption on which the assertion made above is based?

Ⓐ Customers do not have the option of shopping somewhere other than Middle Valley

Ⓑ The other furniture stores in Middle Valley charge more for furniture than does Green's Furniture Warehouse.

Ⓒ The quality of the furniture at Green's Furniture Warehouse is equal to the quality of the furniture in other stores.

Ⓓ Green's Furniture Warehouse is the most cost-effective store in Middle Valley.

Ⓔ Other household items at Green's Furniture Warehouse are also well priced.

Games
Questions 1–4

A city planner is planning the layout of exactly six highway exits: Bainbridge, Crescent, Driscoll, Homer, Kimball, and Morrow. They are all to be placed on the same side of a highway, in positions numbered consecutively from 1 to 6. The arrangement of exits is subject to the following restrictions:

The Bainbridge exit must be placed before the Homer exit.

The Kimball exit must be placed before the Morrow exit.

The Crescent exit cannot be placed in position 1.

The Driscoll exit must be placed next to the Bainbridge exit.

1. Which of the following is an acceptable layout of exits, from positions 1 through 6, according to the restrictions above?

   Ⓐ Morrow, Bainbridge, Driscoll, Kimball, Homer, Crescent

   Ⓑ Crescent, Kimball, Morrow, Driscoll, Bainbridge, Homer

   Ⓒ Kimball, Crescent, Morrow, Homer, Driscoll, Bainbridge

   Ⓓ Bainbridge, Homer, Kimball, Morrow, Crescent, Driscoll

   Ⓔ Driscoll, Bainbridge, Kimball, Crescent, Homer, Morrow

2. If the Crescent exit is placed somewhere after the Homer exit, which of the following must be true?

   Ⓐ The Crescent exit is placed somewhere after the Bainbridge exit.

   Ⓑ The Crescent exit is placed somewhere after the Kimball exit.

   Ⓒ The Crescent exit is placed somewhere after the Morrow exit.

   Ⓓ The Homer exit is placed somewhere before the Kimball exit.

   Ⓔ The Homer exit is placed somewhere before the Driscoll exit.

3. If the Homer exit is placed somewhere before the Kimball exit, the Kimball exit could be placed in which of the following positions?

   Ⓐ 1
   Ⓑ 2
   Ⓒ 3
   Ⓓ 4
   Ⓔ 6

4. If the Morrow exit is placed somewhere before the Bainbridge exit, which of the following must be true?

   Ⓐ The Morrow exit is placed somewhere before the Crescent exit.
   Ⓑ The Morrow exit is placed somewhere before the Driscoll exit.
   Ⓒ The Bainbridge exit is placed somewhere before the Crescent exit.
   Ⓓ The Bainbridge exit is placed somewhere before the Driscoll exit.
   Ⓔ The Bainbridge exit is placed somewhere before the Kimball exit.

Questions 5–7

A two-way messenger system exists between the following departments in a corporation: F and G, F and H, H and K, K and M, K and N, M and J, and J and L.

There is also a one-way messenger system between department J and department G; the possible direction of transit is from J to G.

None of these messenger routes intersect each other except at the departments.

There are no other departments or messenger routes in the corporation

Messengers must follow the direction
established for transit between
departments.

5. To send a message from L to G by messenger, it is necessary for the messenger to travel through department

Ⓐ F
Ⓑ J
Ⓒ K
Ⓓ M
Ⓔ N

6. If a broken elevator temporarily makes the route between H and K unusable, then in order to send a message to F by messenger from N, a messenger would have to go through how many other departments besides F and N?

Ⓐ 2
Ⓑ 3
Ⓒ 4
Ⓓ 5
Ⓔ 6

7. If the hallway between H and K is being resurfaced, making the route unusable, a messenger would NOT be able to travel from

Ⓐ G to F
Ⓑ G to L
Ⓒ J to M
Ⓓ J to L
Ⓔ K to F

A catering company must schedule five different types of events within a seven-day period beginning on a Sunday and ending on the following Saturday. Exactly one event can be scheduled each day. The schedule must conform to the following conditions:

Two banquets are to be scheduled; the second banquet must be scheduled for the fourth day after the day of the first banquet.

Exactly one luncheon is to be scheduled.

Exactly one party is to be scheduled, and the party must be scheduled for either the day before or the day after the day of the first banquet.

Exactly one seminar is to be scheduled, and it must be scheduled on any day before the day of the second banquet.

Exactly one wedding is to be scheduled, and it must be scheduled for the third day after the day of the luncheon.

8. Any of the events could be scheduled for Sunday EXCEPT

   Ⓐ a banquet
   Ⓑ the luncheon
   Ⓒ the party
   Ⓓ the seminar
   Ⓔ the wedding

9. The day on which the luncheon is scheduled must be no more than how many days after the day scheduled for the first banquet?

    Ⓐ 1
    Ⓑ 2
    Ⓒ 3
    Ⓓ 4
    Ⓔ 5

10. If no event is scheduled for Sunday, which of the following could be true?

    Ⓐ The luncheon is scheduled for the day before the day of the first banquet.
    Ⓑ The party is scheduled for the day before the day of the first banquet.
    Ⓒ The seminar is scheduled for the day before the day of the first banquet.
    Ⓓ The wedding is scheduled for the day before the day of the second banquet.
    Ⓔ The wedding is scheduled for the day after the day of the seminar.

PART IV

ANSWERS AND
EXPLANATIONS

VERBAL

Analogies

1. **B**   Make a sentence: A CHOREOGRAPHER creates a DANCE.
(A) Does a connoisseur create art? Nope.
(B) Does a composer create music? Yes.
(C) Does an acrobat create height? Nope.
(D) Does an athlete create contest? Nope.
(E) Does a virtuoso create skill? She has it, but she doesn't create it. (B) is best.

2. **B**   Make a sentence: To SCOWL means to show DISPLEA-SURE. The only answer choice that fits this sentence is choice (B): To kiss means to show affection.

3. **B**   Make a sentence: GOGGLES provide protection for the EYES. The only answer choice that fits this sentence is (B): Gloves provide protection for the hands.

4. **E**   Make a sentence: To DRAWL means to SPEAK slowly. Answer choices (A), (B), and (D) don't fit this sentence. If you weren't sure of the meaning of "scintillate," ask yourself, "Could it mean to flash slowly?" Not likely. And "saunter" does mean to walk slowly. That's (E).

5. **C**   If you're not exactly sure what ARBORETUM means, work backward. Make a sentence for each answer choice and see whether the stem words would fit that sentence.
(A) You could say "A dam holds back the flow of water." Could something hold back the flow of a TREE? No way.
(B) You might say, "A planetarium is a room where the image of a star is projected." Could something be a room where the image of a TREE is projected? Not likely.
(C) Perhaps you're not sure what an apiary is—never eliminate an answer choice when you don't know the meaning of one of the words. (By the way, it's a collection of bee hives.)
(D) You could say, "A museum is place to exhibit a painting." Could something be a place to exhibit a TREE? Possibly.
(E) Your sentence might be "A forum is a public place where a person makes a speech." Could something be a

public place where a person makes a TREE? No chance. The best answer is (C). And a good sentence for the stem words is "An ARBORETUM is a man-made environment where a TREE grows."

6. **D** If you're not sure what GALL means, go right to the answers. Choices (A), (B), (C), and (E) all contain words that are not related to each other, but you'd have to leave in any choices containing words you don't know. In (D), "discomfit" means to cause confusion, and GALL means to cause IRRITATION. Bingo!

7. **A** If you're not sure what a SUBTERFUGE is, go right to the answers and eliminate choices. In (A), are "decanter" and "pour" related? Yes, the function of a decanter is to pour. Could the function of a SUBTERFUGE be to DECEIVE? Sure. Keep this choice. In (B), are "hire" and "interview" related? Try making a sentence . . . no. Eliminate this choice. In (C), are "account" and "save" related? No. Yes, there are such things as "savings accounts," but the words "save" and "account" do not have a relationship to each other (remember, we need *dictionary definitions* in our relationships). Eliminate this choice. In (D), are "outpost" and "protect" related? Not really. Some outposts might be used for protection, but an outpost is really just an outlying settlement. "Protect" is not in the definition of "outpost." Eliminate this choice. In (E), are "film" and "view" related? No. Many other things are viewed besides a film (remember, we need *dictionary definitions* in our relationships). Eliminate this choice. The only answer left is (A), and yes, the function of a SUBTERFUGE is to DECEIVE. That is its *definition*.

8. **C** If you're not sure what RATIFY means, go right to the answers and eliminate choices. Choices (B) and (D) contain words that aren't related to each other. Work backwards on choices (A) and (C): "To mutate is to make a change in nature or form." Could RATIFY mean to make an APPROVAL in nature or form? Not likely. For choice (C), "To duel is to have a formal combat, according to rules." Could to RATIFY mean to have a formal APPROVAL, according to rules? Yes!

9. **E**   SOPORIFIC is a word you need to know for the GRE—ETS loves it. Something soporific causes sleep. That sentence eliminates answer choices (A), (B), (C), and (D). Something astringent does cause a pucker.

10. **C**   If you don't know what METTLESOME means, go right to the answer choices and start eliminating. Answer choices (A), (B) and (E) contain words that are not related to each other, so eliminate them. Then make sentences for the remaining answer choices, and work backward to the stem words. For answer choice (C) your sentence would be "Something ludicrous is characterized by inanity." Could something METTLESOME be characterized by COURAGE? Sure. For choice (D) your sentence would be "Something dubious causes suspiciousness." Could something METTLESOME cause COURAGE? Does *anything* cause COURAGE? Not really.

Sentence Completions

1. **A**   Focus on the second blank. The clue for the second blank is "unable to be accurately forecast." So a good word for the second blank would be "unpredictable." Looking at the second answer-choice words only, that eliminates answer choices (B) and (E). The clue for the first blank is "changing," so the first blank must be a word that's the opposite of the one for the second blank, or "predictable." That eliminates answer choices (C) and (D) and gives us (A).

2. **D**   The clue in the sentence is "Children . . . have become 'hasty viewers.'" The trigger words are "as a result." So a good word for the blank would be "wanders." In any case, it has to be a negative word. The words in answer choices (A), (B), and (E) are positive, and answer choice (C) isn't really negative. That leaves (D).

3. **B**   The clue for the second blank is "the ways in which other businesses might attempt to imitate them." The trigger words are "in order to." So a good word for the second blank would be "highlight." That eliminates answer choices (A), (C), and (D). The clue for the first blank is "the troubles and deficiencies . . . ignored or diminished by the author . . ." So a good word for the first blank would be "intentionally." That eliminates answer choice (E) and leaves (B).

4. **C**   The clue for the second blank is "reproduced repeatedly . . . by long-standing practice." A good word for the second blank would be "approved." Looking only at the second words in the answer choices, you can eliminate answer choices (A), (B), (D), and (E).

5. **A**   The clue for the second blank is "appreciation of the film increased" so the word in the second blank must be positive. Looking only at the second words in the answer choices, you can eliminate answer choices (B), (C), (D), and (E), because the second words in all these choices are negative.

6. **C**   The clue in the sentence is "diverse tastes," so let's put "diversity" in the second blank. That eliminates (A), (B), (D), and (E). It's (C).

7. **B**   The clue for the blank is "daily routines," so the word in the blank can be "routine." That definitely eliminates (A), (D), and (E). If you know what "quotidian" or "recalcitrant" means, you know the answer is (B). If you don't, (C) is a good guess (though wrong).

8. **E**   The clue in the sentence is "led some later thinkers to question." That tells you that there was some problem with the "early metaphysicians' efforts to decipher the workings of the universe." So a good word for the first blank would be "problems." That eliminates answer choices (A), (B), and (C). The second blank must be a word such as "workings," or at least one with positive connotations. That eliminates answer choice (D) and leaves you with (E).

9. **A**   The clue in the sentence is "Being gracious . . . is instead a fundamental virtue." This tells you that the word in the first blank means the opposite of "fundamental virtue," or at least is one with negative connotations. That eliminates answer choices (B), (C), and (D). The virtue of being gracious would be "threatened" by "the fashionable directive to 'say what you feel.'" That eliminates answer choice (E) and leaves (A).

10. **D**   The clue for the first blank is "the purpose of sarcastic remarks is to disturb." So a good word for the first blank would be "disturbances." That eliminates answer choices

(B) and (E). The clue for the second blank is "desire for supremacy in miniature over an environment." So a word for how that environment appears must have negative connotations. That eliminates answer choice (A) (perplexed is negative, but an "environment" can't really appear "perplexed") and (C). You're left with (D).

Antonyms

1. **C** SLUR means to pronounce indistinctly.

2. **E** A MORATORIUM is a period of inactivity.

3. **C** DIFFUSE means to spread out, or disperse.

4. **A** THWART means to prevent from taking place, or to frustrate.

5. **A** AGITATE means to upset or disturb.

6. **E** AUTHENTICATE means to establish as being genuine.

7. **A** ACCLIMATION means an adjustment to a new environment or situation. It's a word with positive connotations, so you could eliminate answer choices that have positive connotations (the opposite of "acclimation" must be a negative word). Answer choices (B), (C), (D), and (E) are all positive words, so they're gone.

8. **A** TENUOUS means insubstantial or flimsy. If you knew only that it was negative, you could eliminate answer choices with negative connotations, like (D) and (E) for sure, and (B), too.

9. **A** FLORID means elaborate in style. If you knew only that it was positive, you could eliminate answer choices (C) and (E), which are positive words. Answer choices (B) and (D) would be good guesses.

10. **E** MISCIBLE means able to be mixed. Hey, it s a tough one. If you don't know the word, just guess and move on.

Reading Comprehension

1. **C**   This is a main idea question, about the passage as a whole. Your "treasure hunt" should have revealed that the passage is basically discussing the way in which Strachey interprets the English women's movement. Eliminate (B) right away because it's not about a "literary" work. Eliminate (D) because it's not a "novel analysis." Eliminate (A) and (E) because they are too specific. That leaves (C).

2. **A**   Go back to the second paragraph, where the book is described. From the first sentence you know it's about "the historical connections between the women's movement and other social and political developments." Sounds like (A).

3. **C**   Since this is an EXCEPT question, you're looking for the choice that the passage does not answer. The passage discussed how Wollstonecraft's political orientation differed from More's, but not how it differed from Strachey's. That's (C).

4. **C**   For line reference questions, go back to the lines cited, and read about five lines before and after those lines. You can find the answer in either place for this question. The first sentence of the paragraph tells us Strachey is writing about "the historical connections between the women's movement and other social and political developments." Choice (C) is just a paraphrase of this.

5. **B**   Look back in the passage for the place where the author "faults" Strachey. It's in the last paragraph, in lines 46–50. The author states, "Where Strachey pictured a relatively fixed image of domestic women throughout the first half of the nineteenth century, recent historical and literary works suggest that this image was both complex and unstable." Sounds like (B).

6. **A**   The author likes Strachey's book, but points out something that Strachey omitted. The attitude is positive, but not overly positive. That's (A). Make sure you know the meaning of the word "qualified" as it's used in this context.

7. **D**   First, go back to the passage to find out what the author said about "the similarity between the English and

American women's movements." It's at the end of the first paragraph. The author says that "like its American counterpart, the English women's movement had a powerful sense of its own historic importance and of its relationship to wider social and political change." So you're looking for an answer choice that would indicate that was not true. Choice (D) directly contradicts the author's assertion.

8. **E** This is a main idea question, about the passage as a whole. Your "treasure hunt" should have revealed that the passage is about how scientists study insects that carry malaria so that those insects could be eradicated. (A) doesn't even mention insects. (C) doesn't mention how scientists study the bugs. (D) doesn't mention eradicating the insects. Since there's no prediction of the future, you can eliminate (B). That leaves (E).

9. **C** Go back to the first paragraph. In lines 7–8 the passage states, "In some localities the mosquito was abundant but malaria rare or absent."

10. **A** Go back to the second sentence of the second paragraph. It says that the mosquito becomes a carrier when it feeds on human blood.

MATH

Numbers

1 **B** First, eliminate (D) because we're only working with numbers here. Don't forget the order of operations, or PEMDAS. Do the 3 + 3 in the inner parentheses first, so you get 4[6 + 4]. Now do the remaining set of parentheses so you get this: 4[10], or 40. So, in Column A, we have 40, and in Column B we have 45. The answer is (B).

2. **A** First, eliminate (D) because we're only working with numbers here. All you have to do here is use the bowtie to compare these fractions. You end up comparing 64 (in Column A) and 63 (in Column B). The answer is (A).

3. **E** Remember the quick test to tell whether a number is divisible by 3? Add up the digits in the number. 1 + 1 + 7 = 9, and, since 9 is divisible by 3, 117 is too. And since 117 is

divisible by 3, there will be no remainder, so the answer is (E).

4. **A**   The units digit in 1,743 is 3. The hundreds digit in 5,243 is 2. The answer is (A).

5. **B**   Let's add those decimals: $1.3 + .6 + .9 = 2.8$. So, $2.8 + x = 5$. Now, $5 - 2.8$ is 2.2, so $x = 2.2$. Column A is 2.2, and Column B is 2.3, so the answer is (B).

6. **A**   When in doubt, expand it out, and don't calculate, because this is quant comp and we only have to compare. In Column A we have (4)(2)(2)(2)(2)(2)(2). In Column B we have (6)(4)(4). Let's break it down even further: Column A is (2)(2)(2)(2)(2)(2)(2)(2), and Column B is (3)(2)(2)(2)(2)(2). Now, get rid of anything both columns have in common. Each column has five 2s, so cross them out. What's left? (2)(2)(2) in Column A and (3) in Column B. In other words, Column A has an 8, and Column B has a 3. The answer is (A).

7. **A**   What would happen if we squared both values? We'd get $\frac{7}{3}$ in Column A and $\frac{1}{9}$ (7) in Column B. Which is bigger, $\frac{7}{3}$ or $\frac{7}{9}$? $\frac{7}{3}$, because it's more than 1 (if you're not sure, use the bowtie to compare them). The answer is (A).

8. **A**   To find the amount Mr. Jones paid in addition to the regular price of the bedroom set, multiply $69 by the 9 months and get $621. Then add the $300 payment. $621 + 300 = 921$. So Mr. Jones paid an additional $21. The $23 in Column A is larger than the $21 in Column B. The answer is (A)

9. **C**   You don't need to multiply 21, 54, and 22. You just need to figure out which fraction in the answer choices has a denominator that K wouldn't be divisible by. How? Well, take a look at (A). For K divided by 21 to be an integer, it would have be divisible by 21; it would have to have 21 as a factor. We know 21 is a factor of K because we're told that $K = (21)(54)(22)$. So we can eliminate (A) because we're looking for the choice that would *not* be an integer. If you look at the rest of the answer choices, you'll notice that none of them mention 21, 54, or 22. Not to worry. If the fac-

tors of K include 21, 54, and 22, they must also include the
factors of 21, 54, and 22. So, other factors of K include 3 and
7, 6 and 9, 3 and 18, and 2 and 11. Any combination of those
numbers will form a factor of K. Now look at (B). For K
divided by 27 to be an integer, it would have to have 27 as a
factor. Well, look at our list of factors, and you'll see a 9 and
a 3, which have a product of 27. That means 27 is a factor of
K, and therefore not the answer. Try (C). For K divided by
48 to be an integer, it would have to have 48 as a factor.
Look at our list of factors. Would any combination of them
give us 48? Nope. That means K divided by 48 is *not* an
integer, and therefore is the answer. By the way, quickly
check out (D) and (E): Can you make 33 with our list of factors? Yes, 11 and 3. Can you make 63? Yes, 9 and 7.

10. **C**   Looks ugly, doesn't it? This is a tough one, but don't worry,
you'd never be expected to calculate these. All we need to
do is compare. Let's start by doing a little factoring to
change the look of these numbers. In Column A, what's the
biggest thing that we can "pull out" of 3^{17} and 3^{18}? We can
divide the whole thing, or "pull out" 3^{17}, so we end up with
$3^{17} (1 + 3^1)$, or $3^{17} (4)$. Looks like Column B, doesn't it? The
answer is (C)

Figures

1. **A**   In a parallelogram, opposite angles are equal, and the big
angle plus the small angle add up to 180 degrees. So $x + 120$
= 180. That makes Column A 60, which is bigger than the 45
in Column B. The answer is (A).

2 **C**   Draw yourself a picture! To find the area of a slice of the
pie, first we need to find the area of the whole pie, then
divide the area of the whole pie by 8 to find the area of each
slice. If the radius of the pie is 6, then the area ($A = \pi r^2$) of
the whole pie would be 36π. Then divide 36π by 8, and you
get $\frac{9}{2} \pi$. That's (C).

3. **B**   To find the perimeter of triangle BCD, first find the length
of BD using the Pythagorean theorem. $5^2 + BD^2 = 13^2$. So
BD = 12. Then you can find the third side of triangle BCD.
$12^2 + DC^2 = 15^2$. Notice that this is a 3:4:5 right triangle. So

DC is 9. Then add up the sides of triangle BCD. $9 + 12 + 15 = 36$. So, Column A is 36. Since Column B is 42, (B) is the answer.

4. **A** A line has 180 degrees, so $a + 20 + b = 180$. That means that $a + b = 160$. We're also told that $a = 3b$, so let's Plug In those answer choices for b to finish this off. (A): $a = 3(40) = 120$. Does $120 + 40 = 160$? Yes. We're done. The answer is (A).

5. **C** To find the value of n, start with the right triangle for which we're given two of the three sides. Use the Pythagorean theorem: $15^2 + b^2 = 25^2$. Notice that this is a 3:4:5 right triangle, since $15 = 3(5)$ and $25 = 5(5)$. So $b = 20$ or $4(5)$. Now we have two of the three sides of the triangle we're interested in: $12^2 + n^2 = 20$. Notice that we've got another 3:4:5 right triangle. $12 = 3(4)$ and $20 = 5(4)$. So $n = 4(4)$ or 16. That's (C).

6. **E** Draw yourself a picture! To find the perimeter of a rectangle, you need to know the length and the width. If the newspaper ad with a width of 14 has the same area as another ad 52 long and 28 wide, that means that 14 (length) = 52(28). Divide both sides by 14, and you get length = 52(2) = 104. So, the dimensions of our mystery ad are $104 + 104 + 14 + 14$. Add them up and you get 236. That's (E).

7. **C** Triangle ABC is isosceles. That means that the base and the height are each equal to 4. So the base of the unshaded region is 3, because the base of the shaded region is 1. The area of triangle ABC is $\frac{1}{2}(4)(4)$, or 8. The area of triangle ABD is $\frac{1}{2}(4)(3)$, or 6. Subtract the area of ABD from the area of ABC to get the area of the shaded region, BCD. That's $8 - 6$, which is 2. So, in Column A, the area of the shaded region, 2, divided by the area of the unshaded region, 6, is $\frac{2}{6}$, or $\frac{1}{3}$. The answer is (C).

8. **B** To find the perimeter of the figure, you need to add up all the sides. To find the missing side of the rectangle, solve for the opposite side of the rectangle, using the Pythagorean theorem: $a^2 + b^2 = c^2$. You may remember that $5^2 + 12^2 = 13^2$. So the missing sides of the rectangle are each 13. Now add

up the sides of the figure: 5 + 12 + 17 + 13 + 17 = 64. That's (B).

9. **B**   Draw yourself a picture! The formula for circumference is $C = \pi d$, also known as $2\pi r$. Since $r = \frac{1}{2}$, $C = (2)\pi \left(\frac{1}{2}\right)$, or π. So we have π in Column A and 4 in Column B. Remember that π is equal to a little more than 3. That means the answer is (B).

10. **A**   Draw yourself a picture! Let's plug in some numbers and see what happens. To start with, make $r = 2$. Then you get $2\pi r = 4\pi$ (which is about 12-ish) in Column A and $4(2) = 8$ in Column B. So Column A is greater if $r = 2$. Eliminate choices (B) and (C). Now let's plug in a weird number; make $r = \frac{1}{2}$. Then you get π in Column A and 2 in Column B. Column A wins again. You can't plug in 0 or a negative number, because r is the radius of the circle and the side of the square. The answer is (A).

Equations I

1. **C**   In Column A, $\frac{30}{100}(150) = \frac{30}{10}(150) = 3(15) = 45$. In Column B, $\frac{60}{100}(75) = \frac{3}{5}(75) = 3(15) = 45$. The answer is (C).

2. **B**   Remember the formula: Average = Total/Number. In this case, we have the average, 17, and the number, 2. That makes the total 34. In other words, the two numbers have to add up to 34, but neither of them can be 12 or less. Since Column A is asking for twice the larger of the two integers, let's figure out what the largest integer could be by pairing it with the smallest integer we can use, or 13. If the total is 34, and one number is 13, that means the other number is 21 because 21 + 13 = 34. So, in Column A, we get 42, which is twice 21. We have 44 in Column B, so (B) is the answer.

3. **D**   First of all, let's do a little ballparking. If a one-hour call costs $7.20, a ten-minute call must cost much less. Eliminate (A). Now let's make a proportion, but first, let's change "one hour" into "60 minutes," since we're comparing it to

ten minutes. So, we have: cost/minutes = $\frac{7.20}{60}$ = $\frac{x}{10}$. A little cross-multiplying gets you $60x = (7.20)(10)$, or $60x = 72$. Divide both sides by 60 and you get $x = 1.20$. That's (D).

4. **C**   Remember the formula: Average = Total/Number. In Column A, the average is $7 + 3 + 4 + 2$, or 16, divided by 4, which is 4. In Column B, we have to find the average of $2a + 5, 4a$, and $7 - 6a$. Why not plug in something for a to make this easier? How about 2? Now we're finding the average of 9, 8, and –5. $9 + 8 - 5 = 12$, divided by the number of numbers, which is 3, gives us 4. So far the answer is (C). Let's plug in again—something weird this time, just to be sure. How about 0? Now we're finding the average of 5, 0, and 7. 12 divided by the number of numbers, which is 3, gives us 4. Again, we get (C). By the way, you could also have solved Column B by adding everything up as is: $2a + 5 + 4a + 7 - 6a = 12$. 12 divided by the number of numbers, which is 3, gives us 4.

5. **C**   It's tempting to think that the two discounts add up to 55 percent. But it just ain't true. Test it out by plugging in the perfect percent number: 100. A 30 percent discount from $100 is $30. If that's followed by a 25 percent, that would be a $25 discount of the $70 remaining dollars. So, 25 percent, or one-fourth, of 70 is $17.50. So p, or the two discounts together, are $30 + $17.50, or $47.50. That's the number in Column B, isn't it? So, the answer is (C).

6. **C**   Remember those quadratic equations? Doesn't $m^2 + 2mn + n^2$ look exactly like $x^2 + 2xy + y^2$ which equals $(x + y)^2$? That means you could rewrite $m^2 + 2mn + n^2$ as $(m + n)^2$. Now, we're also told that $m + n = p$, which means that p and $m + n$ are interchangeable. If we replace the $m + n$ in the $(m + n)^2$ with the p, we get p^2. So, $m^2 + 2mn + n^2 = (m + n)^2 = p^2$. That's (C). Whew! But hey—you can also plug in on this one: let's plug in 2 for m, 3 for n, and 5 for p—we get $2^2 + (2)(2)(3) + 3^2$, which equals 25. That's our target answer. Now, to the answers:

(A) $(4)(5) = 20$. Eliminate.
(B) $15 - 2 = 13$. Eliminate.
(C) $(5)^2 = 25$. Bingo!

7. **E** Don't worry, there's no such thing as a "*". This is one of those funny-symboled function problems. This time, we don't have numbers to use. Sounds like a plug in! Let's plug in $x = 3$ and $y = 2$. First we'll do the $x * y$ in the parentheses. We know that $x * y = x(x - y)$, so $3(3 - 2) = 3(1) = 3$. So, $x * (x * y)$ can be rewritten as $x * 3$. Now, remembering that we made $x = 3$, the question really is $3 * 3 = 3(3 - 3) = 3(0) = 0$. That's the target we're looking for in the answer choices: 0. So let's plug in $x = 3$ and $y = 2$ in the answer choices, and look for 0.

   (A) Does $x^2 - xy = 0$? $(3)^2 - (3)(2) = 9 - 6 = 3$. Nope.
   (B) Does $x^2 - 2xy = 0$? $(3)^2 - 2(3)(2) = 9 - 12 = -3$. Nope.
   (C) Does $x^3 - x^2 - xy = 0$? $(3)^3 - (3)^2 - (3)(2) = 27 - 9 - 6 = 12$. Nope.
   (D) Does $x^3 - (xy)^2 = 0$? $(3)^3 - \{(3)(2)\}^2 = 27 - 36 = -9$. Nope.
   (E) Does $x^2 - x^3 + x^2y = 0$? $(3)^2 - (3)^3 + \{(3)^2(2)\} = 9 - 27 + 18 = 0$. Bingo!

8. **C** Go to the graph and find January 1971 to April 1978. Use Process of Elimination. The greatest amount of private donations to charitable causes for that period was to the category of Child Safety. Eliminate (D). The second greatest was Other. Eliminate choice (E). The third greatest was Environmental Protection. That's (C).

9. **D** This question requires you to find the amount of money received by Child Safety organizations in September 1989 from the left-hand chart. It was $9.4 million. Then divide that amount by the number of Child Safety organizations— 38 (from the right-hand chart). It's time to Ballpark! To make it as easy as possible, round both of those figures up. Pretend it's $10 million divided by 40. That's $250,000. That's (D).

10. **C** Go to the graph and find September 1985 to December 1989. The amount donated to Homeless Aid causes for that period was about $300 million. The amount donated to Animal Rights causes for that period was about $225 million. You can reduce ratios! The ratio of 300:225 reduces to 12:9, or 4:3. That's (C).

Equations II

1　E　Let's Plug In a number for a. How about 10? So, Alex gave Jonathan 10 dollars. She gave Gina two dollars more than she gave Jonathan, so she gave Gina 12 dollars. She gave Louanne three dollars less than she gave Gina, so she gave Louanne 9 dollars. So altogether, Alex gave Gina, Jonathan, and Louanne 10 + 12 + 9, or 31 dollars. (By the way, just ignore that "in terms of a." Because we Plugged In, we're not answering the question in terms of a anymore.) Now let's check the answers, Plugging In 10 for a, and looking for our target answer, 31:

(A)　Does $\dfrac{10}{3}$ = 31? Nope.

(B)　Does 10 – 1 = 31? Nope.

(C)　Does 3(10) = 31? Nope.

(D)　Does 3(10) – 1 = 31? Nope.

(E)　Does 3(10) + 1 = 31? Yes. The answer is (E).

2.　D　You're being told that $3x = -2$, so Plug In –2 for $3x$ in $(3x - 3)2$. This gives you $(-2 - 3)2 = (-5)2 = 25$. That's (D).

3.　D　Which costs more, the car or the paint job? The car. What do the answer choices represent? The cost of the car. Let's Ballpark first. If the combined cost was $4,800, and the biggest chunk of that is the cost of the car, choices (A) and (B) are ridiculously low. A $4,000 paint job for an $800 car? No way. Eliminate those choices. What choices are left? (C), (D), and (E). Start plugging in the middle of those values, (D), $4,000. Hey, it's also the easiest number to work with, so why not? We're told that the cost of the paint job was $\dfrac{1}{5}$ the cost of the car. One-fifth of $4,000 is $800 (now we see where that trap answer choice came from). Is $4,000 plus $800 equal to $4,800? Yes. We're done—the answer is (D).

4.　E　Start with $x = y$. Let's Plug In 4 for both x and y. Now put that into the first equation to get z; 4 + 4 = 8, so $z = 8$. Now let's go to the answers, Plugging In 4 for x and y and 8 for z:

(A)　2(4) + 2(4) = 2(8). 8 + 8 = 16. That's true.

(B)　4 – 4 = 0. That's true.

(C) $4 - 8 = 4 - 8$. That's true.

(D) $4 = \dfrac{8}{2}$. That's true.

(E) $4 - 4 = 2(8)$. $0 = 16$? That's not true, and since this is an EXCEPT question, (E) is the answer.

5. **A** Let's Plug In 2 for x and 3 for y—that makes xy an even integer.

(A) $(2)(3) + 5 = 11$. That's odd, so leave it in.

(B) $2 + 3 = 5$. That's odd, so leave it in.

(C) $\dfrac{2}{3}$. That's not an integer, so eliminate it.

(D) $4(2) = 8$. That's even, so eliminate it.

(E) $7(2)(3) = 42$. That's even, so eliminate it.

So, we got rid of choices (C), (D), and (E). But standard operating procedure on a "must be" question says we need to Plug In twice; otherwise, how would we choose between (A) and (B)? At first we made x even and y odd. Let's make them both even and just change y to 4. Is xy even, using these numbers? Yes, it's 8. Now let's go back to the two remaining choices.

(A) $(2)(3) + 5 = 13$. That's still odd, so leave it in.

(B) $2 + 4 = 6$. That's even, so eliminate it. The answer is (A).

6. **C** Use those answer choices! Since the question is asking for the least number, start by Plugging In (A), the least number in the answer choices.

(A) Does $\{3(-3) + 2\} \{-3 - 3\} = 0$? $(-7)(-6) = -42$, which isn't 0.

(B) Does $\{3(-2) + 2\} \{-2 - 2\} = 0$? $(-4)(-4) = -16$, which isn't 0.

(C) Does $\{3(-\dfrac{2}{3}) + 2\} \{-\dfrac{2}{3} - 3\} = 0$? $(0)(-3\dfrac{2}{3}) = 0$. Bingo!

7. **D** First Plug In an easy number. How about $x = 2$? That gives us 3 as the quantity in Column A and -1 as the quantity in Column B. We know that 3 is greater than -1; *so far* the answer is (A). Eliminate (B) and (C) on your scratch paper. For our second round of Plugging In, try $x = 0$. That gives us 1 in Column A and 1 in Column B—now the two columns are equal. We Plugged In *different* numbers, we got *different* answers. Therefore, the answer is (D).

8. **B**   The information about tips is the catch. Its only purpose is to cause careless errors. Confront this trap by reducing the day's total by $20—to $160. What we're left with is a very straightforward problem. If each customer bought 2 four-dollar dishes, then each customer spent $8 on food. Now you can plug in the answer choices:
(A) Does 18 equal 160 divided by 8? Nope.
(B) Does 20 equal 160 divided by 8? Yes.
(C) Does 22 equal 160 divided by 8? Nope.
(D) Does 40 equal 160 divided by 8? Nope.
(E) Does 44 equal 160 divided by 8? Nope.

By the way, you also could have divided $160 by $8 to get 20. The answer is (B).

9. **C**   Don't forget to Plug In on geometry problems with variables. Plugging In according to the rule of 180, we can make $a = 50$, and make the other two angles inside the triangle 60 and 70. Because b and c are vertical to the other angles in the triangle, $b + c = 130$ in Column A. $180 - 50 = 130$ in Column B. The answer is (C).

10. **C**   With all of these percents, wouldn't it be nice to have a total number? Just plug one in. Let's make the total number of voters 100 (the best number to Plug In when you're dealing with percents). 60 percent of the voters are women, so that's 60 women, and the remaining voters are men, so that's 40 (we made the total 100, remember?) men. 30 percent of the women would be 30 percent of 60, which is $\frac{30}{100}(60)$, or 18 women, who voted for Candidate X. 20 percent of the men would be 20 percent of 40, which is $\frac{20}{100}(40)$, or 8 men, who voted for candidate X. So, the total number of people voting for candidate X is 18 + 8, or 26. Since our total is 100, 26 is equal to 26 percent. That's (C).

ANALYTIC

Arguments

1. **C**   The conclusion is that Clean toothpaste doesn't prevent tooth decay, and we need to weaken that.
(A) Willingness to switch is outside the scope.
(B) What the ads say is outside the scope.
(C) So, the tooth decay problem would be even worse without Clean toothpaste. That means the toothpaste must be helping a little. Bingo!
(D) Dentist recommendations are outside the scope.
(E) Gum disease is outside the scope.

2. **A**   The last sentence of the argument is the conclusion: "... when Rogerton's zoo reopens next year, either Stilton or Bailey will have to be closed and their animal populations consolidated." An assumption must support the conclusion that one of those zoos will have to be closed.
(A) If one of those zoos is left underpopulated, that's a reason to close it. That supports the argument. Bingo!
(B) This implies that some animals might have to stay at Bailey or Stilton, which hurts the argument.
(C) If the Rogerton animals are only a small part of the zoo populations, Bailey or Stilton probably won't have to be closed, which hurts the argument.
(D) Resources are outside the scope.
(E) Animals sent between the zoos are outside the scope.

3. **A**   This is an inference question, so we need something that we know *must* be true, based on the argument. All we know so far is that the high-protein, low-fat diet didn't seem to affect blood pressure any differently than the low-protein, high-fat diet did.
(A) That's true, since the high-protein, low-fat diet didn't seem to affect blood pressure. Bingo!
(B) We don't know if they're representative or not.
(C) We don't know what some physicians believe
(D) We don't know this about vegetarians, and besides they are out of the scope of the argument.
(E) This goes against the argument, because the argument

seems to be implying that there's no link between protein intake and high blood pressure.

4. **B** We have to support the conclusion, which is that Main Street Laundromat is cleaner because of the amount of water the machines use.

(A) This is already mentioned in the argument, so it doesn't help—it doesn't add anything new.

(B) This takes away the possibility that the reason the clothes were cleaner from Main Street was because Joe used a different detergent there, thereby strengthening the argument that it's the water. Bingo!

(C) This contradicts the argument, so it doesn't help.

(D) How much laundry Joe does is outside the scope. We only care how clean the clothes are.

(E) How dirty Joe's clothes were is outside the scope. We only care how clean the clothes *turned out*.

5. **D** The conclusion is that the man-made hormone wards off insect infestation, just because there aren't any in the section. We have to weaken this by coming up with another reason there aren't any insects in that section.

(A) Even if the dearth wasn't complete, it still doesn't explain why there was any dearth at all.

(B) So we need to add more. Does this affect whether it's working or not?

(C) Out of scope. We only care about *this* hormone.

(D) So there might be another reason for the dearth, other than the hormone. That undermines the argument. Bingo!

(E) It may not compensate for the plant loss in that section, but that doesn't explain why there was any dearth at all.

6. **E** Remember that an inference is something that is known to be true, based on what you're told in the argument. For inference questions, go with the safest, least disputable answer choice that you *know* is true.

(A) We can't predict the future, so we don't know this.

(B) The phrase "will not be discovered" is too extreme.

(C) The phrase "will not function safely" is too extreme.

(D) The phrase "will have to be designed" is too extreme.

(E) Yes, the safety can't be ensured; in other words, we're not sure it's safe. Bingo!

7. **B**   The discrepancy we have to explain is that the percentages don't seem to match up.
(A) This doesn't mention gender, so it won't explain anything.
(B) This explains the apparent discrepancy by revealing that many of the judges got the position before the fifteen-year time frame the argument discusses. Bingo!
(C) Specializing is outside the scope.
(D) Salaries are outside the scope.
(E) Circuit judgeships are outside the scope.

8. **B**   The argument draws an analogy between fighting infectious diseases and attempts at pest control.
(A) We're looking for pest control.
(B) Pest control. Bingo!
(C) We're looking for pest control.
(D) We're looking for pest control.
(E) We're looking for pest control.

9. **A**   The claim is that collies are popular because of their performances at dog shows. To weaken that, we need an alternate cause, some other reason that collies are popular that has nothing to do with dog shows.
(A) This gives another reason for collies' popularity as pets, one that wouldn't be apparent from a dog show. Bingo!
(B) This is about dog shows; we need some other reason for the popularity of collies.
(C) Public interest is outside the scope.
(D) Schnauzers are outside the scope.
(E) This is about dog shows; we need some other reason for the popularity of collies.

10. **B**   The premise is that no store charges less than Green's, which doesn't say anything about stores that charge *the same* as Green's. The conclusion is that Green's has the lowest prices.
(A) Shopping elsewhere in the valley is outside the scope. We only care about Middle Valley.
(B) This eliminates the possibility that any stores charge *the same* as Green's. Bingo!
(C) Quality is outside the scope. We only care about price.
(D) Cost-effectiveness is outside the scope. We only care about price.

(E) Other household items are outside the scope. We only care about furniture.

Games

1. **E** First of all, here's what your diagram should look like:

BCDHKM

B...H

K...M

~H
~M   ~B
~C   ~K

| DB | / | BD |

| 1 | 2 | 3 | 4 | 5 | 6 |

For this question, systematically eliminate choices by using your clues. First, B must be somewhere to the left of H, so eliminate (C). Next, K must be somewhere to the left of M, so eliminate (A). Next, C can't be in 1, so eliminate (B). Next, there's a DB/BD block, so eliminate (D). That leaves us with (E).

2. **A** C must come somewhere to the right of H, which is already coming to the right of B. If C is placed after H, and B must be before H, then C must be after B: B ... H ... C. That's (A).

3. **D** H, which is somewhere to the right of B, is now somewhere to the left of K, which is already somewhere to the left of M: B ... H ... K ... M. We're trying to figure out where K must be placed. If at least M must come after it, K can't be sixth, so eliminate (E). If at least B (and D, because of the BD block), and H must come after it, K can't be first, second, or third. That eliminates (A), (B), and (C). We're left with (D). Draw it out if you're not sure.

4. B Now M is somewhere to the left of B, which is already somewhere to the left of H. Also, M is already somewhere to the right of K: K...M..B...H. Let's draw some pictures:

~H
~M   ~B
~C   ~K

	1	2	3	4	5	6
④	K	M	B	D	H	C
	K	M	D	B	H	C
	K	C	M	B	D	H
	K	C	M	D	B	H

Now check the answers. The only one that's true in all cases is (B).

5. B First of all, here's what you're diagram might look like:

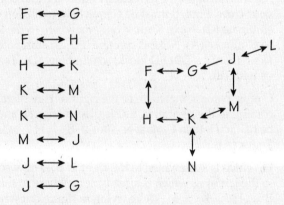

F ⟷ G

F ⟷ H

H ⟷ K

K ⟷ M

K ⟷ N

M ⟷ J

J ⟶ L

J ⟷ G

Don't worry if it doesn't look *exactly* like this, as long as the connections are all the same. Now, the question asks us to go from L to G. The path is L ⟶ J ⟶ G. The messenger must travel through J. That's (B).

6. **C**   Use the same diagram, and just cover up the connection between H and K. Here's the path to get from N to F:

$$N \longrightarrow K \longrightarrow M \longrightarrow J \longrightarrow G \longrightarrow F.$$ Besides N and F, we went through four departments. That's (C).

7. **B**   As in the previous question, cover up the connection between H and K. Now check the answers.
(A) Can we still go from G to F? Yes. Eliminate it.
(B) Can we still go from G to L? No. Remember, you can only go from J to G, not from G to J. So you can't go from G to L without going all the way around, which we can no longer do without the H-K connection.
(C) Can we still go from J to M? Yes. Eliminate it.
(D) Can we still go from J to L? Yes. Eliminate it.
(E) Can we still go from K to F? Yes. Eliminate it.

8. **E**   First, your diagram should look like this:

See all those deductions on top of the diagram? They all came from the clues. Clues about order will almost always yield deductions like these. Notice also that though there are seven days, there are only six elements. That's why we listed an X with the elements—to represent the "empty" element-less day. Now, the question is about what can't happen on Sunday. Look at the top of the diagram: W can't be there (because it has to come after the luncheon). That's (E).

9. **C**   Let's try to make the luncheon as many days after the first banquet as we can, noticing the restrictions on the top of the diagram (that L can't be on Thursday, Friday, or Saturday because it has to be three days before the wedding):

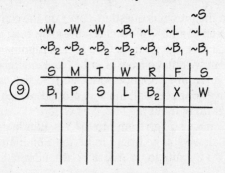

The luncheon is, at most, three days after the first banquet. That's (C).

10. **A**   The only way to handle this "could" question is to try out each answer choice to see if it's possible, remembering to put the X in at Sunday. Let's try (A), the luncheon is scheduled for the day before the day of the first banquet:

			~S			
~W	~W	~W	~B_1	~L	~L	~L
~B_2	~B_2	~B_2	~B_2	~B_1	~B_1	~B_1
S	M	T	W	R	F	S

	S	M	T	W	R	F	S
⑨	B_1	P	S	L	B_2	X	W
⑩	X	L	B_1	P	W	S	B_2

Hey, it works. It could be true, because it doesn't violate any conditions. The answer is (A).

ABOUT THE AUTHOR

Karen Lurie is the author of five books, including *Cracking the GRE CAT* and the *LSAT/GRE Analytic Workout*. She lives in New York City.

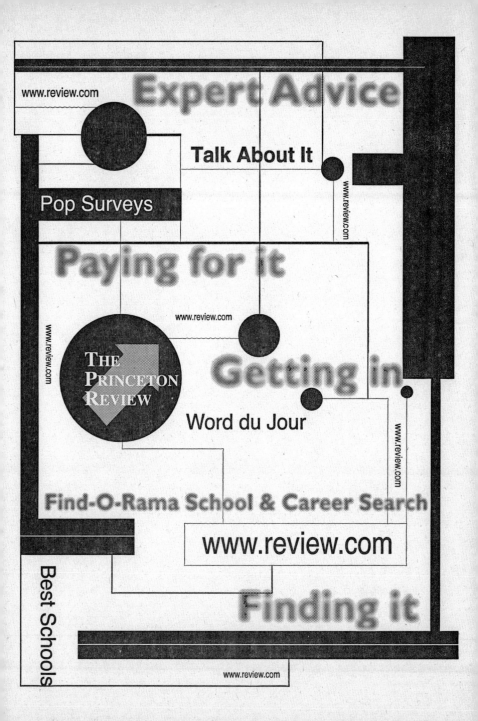

FIND US...

International

Hong Kong
4/F Sun Hung Kai Centre
30 Harbour Road, Wan Chai,
Hong Kong
Tel: (011)85-2-517-3016

Japan
Fuji Building 40, 15-14
Sakuragaokacho, Shibuya Ku,
Tokyo 150, Japan
Tel: (011)81-3-3463-1343

Korea
Tae Young Bldg, 944-24,
Daechi- Dong, Kangnam-Ku
The Princeton Review- ANC
Seoul, Korea 135-280,
South Korea
Tel: (011)82-2-554-7763

Mexico City
PR Mex S De RL De Cv
Guanajuato 228 Col. Roma
06700 Mexico D.F., Mexico
Tel: 525-564-9468

Montreal
666 Sherbrooke St.
West, Suite 202
Montreal, QC H3A 1E7 Canada
Tel: (514) 499-0870

Pakistan
1 Bawa Park - 90 Upper Mall
Lahore, Pakistan
Tel: (011)92-42-571-2315

Spain
Pza. Castilla, 3 - 5° A, 28046
Madrid, Spain
Tel: (011)341-323-4212

Taiwan
155 Chung Hsiao East Road
Section 4 - 4th Floor,
Taipei R.O.C., Taiwan
Tel: (011)886-2-751-1243

Thailand
Building One, 99 Wireless Road
Bangkok, Thailand 10330
Tel: (662) 256-7080

Toronto
1240 Bay Street, Suite 300
Toronto M5R 2A7 Canada
Tel: (800) 495-7737
Tel: (716) 839-4391

Vancouver
4212 University Way NE,
Suite 204
Seattle, WA 98105
Tel: (206) 548-1100

National (U.S.)

We have over 60 offices around the U.S. and
run courses in over 400 sites. For courses and locations
within the U.S. call 1 (800) 2/Review and you will be
routed to the nearest office.